James O. Hacker, Jr., MS
Don C. Dodson, PhD
M. Thane Forthman, MBA

A Marketing Approach to Physician Recruitment

Pre-publication
REVIEWS,
COMMENTARIES,
EVALUATIONS . . .

"**I** would strongly recommend *A Marketing Approach to Physician Recruitment* to anyone who is recruiting physicians. It is current and does an excellent job of pulling all the tips, references, and legalities together in one convenient package.

I have been devoting approximately 50 percent of my time over the last four years to physician recruiting. During that time, I spent at least 30 percent of my recruiting time learning the skills, methods, legalities, etc., that are contained in this book. Imagine how much time I could have saved by starting with a reference book like this!

I have attended numerous lectures and seminars, and read countless articles, all of which have left me with no more information than is contained in this one book!"

Jim Reid, MBA,
Administrative Director
for Professional Development,
AMI Piedmont Medical Center,
Rock Hill, South Carolina

The Haworth Press, Inc.

A Marketing Approach to Physician Recruitment

HAWORTH Marketing Resources
Innovations in Practice & Professional Services
William J. Winston, Senior Editor

New, Recent, and Forthcoming Titles:

A Marketing Approach to Physician Recruitment

James O. Hacker, Jr., MS
Don C. Dodson, PhD
M. Thane Forthman, MBA

The Haworth Press
New York • London • Norwood (Australia)

The Haworth Press, Inc., 10 Alice Street, Binghamton, NY 13904-1580

Library of Congress Cataloging-in-Publication Data

Hacker, James O.
   A marketing approach to physician recruitment / James O. Hacker, Don C. Dodson, M. Thane Forthman.
       p.   cm. – (Haworth marketing resources)
   Includes bibliographical references and index.
   ISBN 1-56024-899-8 (acid-free paper).
   1. Physicians–United States–Recruiting. I. Dodson, Don C. II. Forthman, M. Thane. III. Title.
IV. Series.
RA972.H23   1994
610'.68'3–dc20   93-41669
                                                                                                        CIP

CONTENTS

ABOUT THE AUTHORS

James O. Hacker, Jr., MS, brings eighteen years of physician recruiting, marketing, and planning experience to this book. Vice President of The Health Service Group and Director of the Health Administration Program at Winthrop University in Rock Hill, SC, he consults with healthcare organizations, Healthcare Delivery Systems, and physicians' practices. Mr. Hacker has a successful record of developing recruiting programs, integrated healthcare delivery systems, and medical staff development strategic planning.

Don C. Dodson, PhD, is Director of the Health Administration Programs at Pfeiffer College-Charlotte, Charlotte, NC. He is a former Executive Director of the American Academy of Health Administration and is the founding editor of the *Journal of Health Care Marketing*. In addition, Dr. Dodson has written over 50 articles and has been an author or contributor to five books.

M. Thane Forthman, MBA, Principal of Sales and Marketing, is responsible for the management of the sales and consulting staff for HCIA's Provider Market. Mr. Forthman has extensive experience consulting with hospital administrative and medical staffs to improve financial and quality performance. Over the past few years he has been involved with numerous hospitals, management companies, and consulting firms to affect positive, quantified results in the delivery of efficient and effective healthcare.

Foreword

The healthcare industry is experiencing a new awareness of its role within the community it serves as well as the need to realign its internal priorities.

No longer can it be totally dependent upon the public to seek it out or count on glitzy advertising to bring the masses to its doorstep. It is finding it must be a part of its community as a contributing citizen and as a leader willing to take risks in a non-traditional sense by advocating health policy and actively identifying what the public needs and wants.

Within itself, it is learning that it must be a more integrated system where activities do not stop at department borderlines but continue uninterrupted and smoothly from the patient and customer viewpoint. The increasing sophistication of purchasers of services, whether they be government entities or other managed care players, is leading them to choose well-integrated systems capable of delivering a favorably priced service at a level of quality that satisfies the purchaser.

The traditional, distinctive, three-legged stool of board, medical staff, and hospital is becoming a blended concept–each with its own individual tasks, but each more highly dependent on the others for the success of the whole.

The winners have learned the lessons; the current survivors are either making the transition necessary to become winners, or remaining stuck, eventually becoming a part of a group where "lessons are learned."

A variety of concepts is becoming interwoven into our systems, including systems-thinking and total quality management.

The quality of the medical staff and the number of specialties included are fundamental components of health care that have been largely left to chance. As an integrated system that is going to win, neither the individual provider nor the system as a whole can permit its physician profile to be ignored. There has got to be the right mix to meet the needs of the community, including the strategic plan of the health system as it becomes more driven toward managed care and more reliant upon preventive and outpatient services, and forges necessary partnerships.

As systems begin addressing their physician-component needs, and the medical staff becomes a part of the process of planning its future, this book serves as a comprehensive reference for adding to the physician resource pool, whether it be for expansion of a small group practice, a free-standing hospital, or a multi-institutional system.

The material is comprehensive and well laid out to enable anyone to use it effectively, whether the reader is a sole practitioner, a large medical group, a small single hospital, or an integrated hospital system. The material is instructive for starting a recruitment program or for fine-tuning an existing one.

Bryan Ballard, CEO
South Valley Hospital
Gilroy, California

Chapter 1

Physician Recruitment

Physician recruiting has become a core medical staff development program initiated by hospitals. Physician recruiting is necessary to maintain the hospital levels of utilization, develop new service lines, support new technologies, and expand market share.

Chapter 1 investigates the issues that have made medical physician recruiting so critical to the success of a hospital. The current healthcare marketplace has been analyzed and specific issues have been addressed including the maldistribution of physicians, the trends now faced by physicians and hospitals, and the current concerns about the Graduate Medical Education National Advisory Committee (GMENAC) report and the physician population issues which that report raised.

Physician recruitment, like any other management process, needs to be well planned. The implementation of a well-thought-out and effective physician recruitment strategic plan will address the needs of the community for additional physicians, gain medical staff support for recruiting efforts, match physician recruitment with the hospital's strategic plan and develop tactics for the projected physician recruitment needs of the hospital. Specifically, a recruitment plan will address the hospital's future physician needs for replacing those physicians who retire or move. The Physician Recruitment Plan will also identify and project population changes and their affect on the hospital's physician mix. In addition, the Strategic Physician Recruitment Plan will project growth in managed care contracts, direct contracting and the physician mix needed to adequately support the additional patients brought in through those contracts.

To be competitive, the hospital must continually develop new services and technology to meet the changing needs of both the consumer and the physician markets. New technology and services will demand additional physicians with specific expertise.

There are several specific objectives of the Strategic Recruitment Plan. The first is to maintain the present medical staff by replacement of those physicians who are either retiring or moving away or who have reached that point within their practice life cycles where they are starting to see fewer patients. A second objective is to penetrate and control new markets, either through geographic placement of new physicians or by bringing in a physician of a specific specialty. Another objective is to develop new service lines, and only through recruitment of physicians who have specific expertise can new service lines be implemented and maintained. The fourth objective is to support the existing medical staff by assisting physicians and/or group practices in the recruitment of additional physicians in order to expand the practice.

Another very important objective is to gain support from the medical staff with the implementation of a well-thought-out Strategic Recruitment Plan. A plan in which the existing medical staff has played a role in its development and implementation will be more readily accepted than recruitment without any specific plan or input from the medical staff. Physician recruitment is also necessary due to the increased importance of managed care contracting. It is necessary that the hospital have a core of physicians who will co-negotiate and co-treat managed care patients.

In 1980, the Graduate Medical Education National Advisory Committee, better known as GMENAC, predicted that by 1990 there would be a 70,000 physician surplus and recommended that medical schools decrease their enrollment. There was, in fact, a decrease in enrollment for the six years from 1983 to 1989.

However, the GMENAC report failed to consider several factors. These factors have seriously affected the initial predictions of that report and some healthcare experts are concerned about a shortage of physicians in the near future. In rural areas significant physician shortages now exist. The GMENAC report failed to foresee a maldistribution of physicians away from rural facilities, concentrated in urban centers and away from primary care. It also did not foresee the concentration of specialists and sub-specialists.

The American College of Medical Staff Affairs (*The Medical Staff Affairs Institute* published October 1, 1988), indicated several trends that will affect the practice of medicine in the future and consequently will affect the ability of the healthcare organization to recruit and retain new physicians to provide alternatives to the traditional practice of medicine. The issues affecting medical staff affairs are:

The decline of fee for service.

In 1990 the American Medical Association reported that there are now more salaried physicians than fee-for-service physicians. This trend reflects an increased demand by physicians for financial security and the desire to be released from administrative responsibilities. This trend also indicates the continuing increase in group practices. The AMA recently reported that "Solo practitioners have declined from 43.3% of all non-federal physicians in 1984 to only 38.5% in 1985." At the same time the number of group practices has increased from 10,762 in 1980 to 17,680 in 1988.

There has been a change in the attitude of the physician and more physicians are now willing to practice within a managed care setting or to work for a corporate entity.

The decline of traditional primary care medicine with a greater emphasis on technological specialties.

Several factors have dissuaded potential physicians from entering primary care. Primary care physicians are compensated less than specialty physicians. As a primary care physician there are greater time demands, thereby reducing the amount of time that a physician has for personal activities. The growth and specialization of technology have made it more difficult for a physician to be a generalist.

Income reduction for all physicians. Competition has given group practices or alliances of physicians an economic advantage.

With increased competition and emphasis on cost containment, physicians today have seen a stagnation in their incomes.

The solo practitioner is at a distinct economic disadvantage because group practices have greater long-term control of referrals with the ability to internally refer patients from primary care to specialty care and back. Group practices also have greater economies of scale. Fixed costs are spread among more physicians. Solo practitioners have more limited use and availability of technologies while group practices or alliances have the ability to purchase technology and also possess physician specialties within the group practice to utilize that technology. A solo practitioner must absorb all liabilities and risk of practicing medicine while a group practice can spread the liability and risk of practice among all the group members. Politically the solo practitioner does not have the impact that a group practice has, simply because of scale. A single practitioner will not economically impact a healthcare organization as a group practice will.

Segmentation of medical practices to develop market niches.

This is brought about by the necessity for the practice to uniquely position itself within the marketplace. Such position is necessitated because there is the need to adapt to specific patient demographic or psychographic segments. As an example, a urologist may perceive a need for developing an impotency clinic or a psychiatrist may see the need for opening a depression clinic. Such a practice would be identifying a specific need and filling that need by developing a new service. As the population changes (due to geographic location, or the aging population with the increased probability of a higher Medicaid or Medicare payor mix), the practice may wish to develop services or position itself to appeal to an entirely different payor mix. As an example, a family practitioner or an internist who is located in a more urban setting, may realize that his practice is becoming heavily dependent on federal or state reimbursement. The practice may then perceive the need to change its payor mix and identify itself as a practice developing a medicine service or contracting for episodic care targeted toward local businesses.

A practice may wish to position itself to take advantage of a physician's unique clinical qualifications. As an example, a group practice may have recently hired a gerontologist or an OB/GYN group may have recently hired a physician who has expertise in infertility. Because of an influx of new physicians, or a demographic change in the population, the practice services or the necessity for the practice to develop a direct contracting service, are simply indications that the practice has adapted to changing market factors. Meeting competition is an extremely important reason for the practice to develop a market niche. Ophthalmologists whose competitors are promoting *one stitch or no stitch surgery* must adapt themselves and identify special expertise simply to maintain competitive parity with other ophthalmologists.

As practices acquire more technology within their offices, the technology itself can be critical to the positioning of the practice. An example is the practice that purchases machinery to test for peripheral vascular disease. Another criterion to the development of market niches is the ability of the practice to fill an unmet need. An example would be a physician who identifies either a specific demographic group or geographic area that is either under-served or needs the development of new services.

The erosion of physician/patient relationships under Managed Care/Contract Services.

Managed Care will have the ultimate responsibility of directing patients to either the Contract Physicians or those physicians who belong to the Managed Care IPA. A form of conflict that will arise is the Managed Care's determination to direct patients toward more preventive care even though healthcare in the United States is targeted more toward acute or symptomatic care. Also, cost containment efforts also are forcing patients to pay more out-of-pocket cost and directing them away from some medical procedures.

Now, more than ever, the Managed Care payors are having the ultimate say in how much healthcare will be delivered to a specific patient. In addition, there are conflicts between the payors and the physicians concerning the definition of quality of care. Physicians typically identify *quality of care* thus: "as much care as they feel needs to be provided." Third-party payors and Managed Care, on the other hand, define *quality of care* as "enough care needed to bring a patient to a certain point on a cure continuum." There will also be conflicts between payors and physicians when a referral or a procedure is recommended that will not be reimbursed.

Greater emphasis upon uniform practice patterns.

The third-party payors will demand universal practice patterns as a standardized measure of effectiveness for quality and outcomes. The greater power of the third-party payors to control practice patterns will also standardize medicine because they control reimbursement. Ultimately, universal Diagnosis Related Group (DRG)-like systems for physician reimbursement will be implemented by third-party payors. This will further standardize reimbursement and affect the utilization of technology. Third-party payors will begin to measure physicians based on their outcomes.

There will be restriction at different levels of patient care consequences of rationing medical care.

As reimbursement issues become more critical, there will tend to become a secondary and tertiary level of patients, those who are on Medicaid and/or Medicare and those who are indigent. These patients will have varying levels of care which will range from basic to practically no care at all.

Healthcare providers, the physicians and the hospitals, will find themselves in the precarious position of claiming to provide quality of care while turning away patients. Today in the United States there are 37 million people who do not have healthcare insurance. A larger portion of these individuals are employed but they work for small companies who have found the cost of healthcare insurance prohibitive and have opted not to provide insurance for their employees. Consequently, as the pool of paying patients becomes smaller and smaller, because of the issues of aging and under-insured or uninsured and indigent patients, physicians and hospitals will find themselves spending more and more money in the attempt to appeal to a smaller and smaller patient base while virtually ignoring those who have restrictions on their reimbursement or who are unable to reimburse at all.

Consequently, physicians and hospitals find themselves competing on a technological, quality, and service level in an ever increasingly energetic attempt to gain more market share of those patients who can pay their bills or who are insured. Physician recruitment plays a major role in assisting the physician, group practices, and hospitals in gaining the necessary staffing to penetrate more lucrative markets, establish technological centers of excellence, gain market share, and compete more effectively within this ever-tightening marketplace.

* * *

The 1992 elections where a Democratic President and Congress were elected portends a significant change in the delivery of healthcare within the United States. The direction seems to be toward more state and/or Federal regulation and greater emphasis on cost containment with concurrent emphasis on quality–specifically, either through the structure, the process, or outcomes of healthcare. The emphasis will be either on managed competition, single payor, or on the issue of "play or pay." Specifically, either an employer plays and provides employees with a healthcare plan, or the employer pays by paying a tax that will cover non-insured employees. This "play or pay" scenario will tend to drive smaller employers into either developing coalitions or seeking alternative forms of providing healthcare for their employees. Therein lies a critical issue of physician recruitment. The healthcare facility must have medical staff willing to join with the healthcare facility in developing managed care contracts or direct contracting.

Chapter 2

The Physician Recruitment Planning Process

The recruiting function is a sales function based on the establishment of several goals, specifically the goal of acquiring physicians' résumés, developing site visits, and the actual recruitment of the physician.

Chapter 2 develops an outline for the strategic recruitment plan providing a sequential process for the recruitment of physicians. This plan addresses the issues of hospitals' recruitment needs, the medical staff's concerns and need for specialty support, and the community's needs. Physician-to population ratios are provided as a guide for recruiting specific specialties. Other areas addressed are population growth and movement, the recruiting facility's market share, and ways to calculate the profitability of each physician recruited.

Until the early to mid-1980s, hospitals, unless they were located in very rural areas, did not accept the responsibility for medical staff relations and physician recruitment. Several reasons existed for hospitals not actively recruiting physicians.

- Based on projections, there would be more than enough physicians–in fact a glut–to practice medicine.

- Physician recruitment was seen as the responsibility of the medical staff.

- Hospital Administrators were concerned about criticism from their medical staffs if they actively recruited additional physicians.

- The consuming public–not the physician–was seen as the hospital's primary market.

By the mid- to late 1980s, attitudes had changed significantly. These changes were caused by two factors: DRG's were now in place and hospitals were feeling the squeeze caused by falling reimbursement.

- Competing free-standing health facilities were becoming more prevalent.

- The competition within healthcare was heating up.

- Physicians were not as plentiful as first thought and there were the first murmurs of a possible physician shortage.

- Hospitals became more dependent on government reimbursement.

- Managed Care further drove down reimbursement levels.

- By 1989, over 80% of the hospitals in the United States were recruiting physicians.

- For the first time in history, there were more salaried physicians than fee-for-service physicians.

- Hospital marketing efforts were being shifted away from the public and targeted toward the physician.

The changing healthcare market has driven hospitals to seek a closer working relationship with their medical staff. In addition, physician recruitment has become an important management responsibility in a physician relations strategy.

To be effective, a Physician Recruitment Plan should investigate three areas:

1. Hospital recruitment needs.
2. Medical staff concerns and desires.
3. Community needs and attitudes about healthcare delivery.

The recruitment plan should start with an investigation of the hospital, specifically, the administration and department heads. Interviews should center on the following issues:

1. Projected new services or technology.
2. Current and projected staffing levels.
3. Review of the medical staff bylaws.
4. Current market share information.
5. An investigation of competitive activities in surrounding service areas and within the community itself.
6. An investigation of physician activities as measured against national norms.

The medical staff will also be interviewed. These interviews will center on the following topics:

1. Physician-to-physician relations.
2. Hospital-to-physician relations.
3. The necessity of recruiting for specific physician specialties, or to bolster a solo practitioner or a group practice.
4. Services or technologies that the hospital should add within the near future.

To assist the hospital in developing effective market information, statistical information should be gathered from national, state and local agencies and the hospital's data base. This information is used to investigate the following:

1. The physician ages and specialty mix.
2. Discharges by physician.
3. Discharges by physician specialty.
4. Average age by physician specialty.
5. Revenue by physician and specialty, indicating the level of revenues by physicians for Medicare and Medicaid reimbursement.
6. Top physicians by discharge and revenue.
7. Out-patient utilization by each physician.
8. Identification of the hospitals where the physicians practice.
9. Comparison of the medical staff physicians to national averages for:

   • Average revenue per admission/discharge.
   • Inpatient revenue by specialty compared to national averages.

- Distribution of admissions/discharge by specialty compared to national averages.

10. Discharge distribution by physician and specialty.
11. Length of stay by specialty.
12. Analysis of practice life cycles.

The practice life cycle indicates whether the physician is entering practice, has reached a plateau, or is in the declining years of practice.

It is strongly suggested that an analysis of the community be conducted. This analysis would include focus groups that are composed of individuals who sought healthcare and were treated within the hospital's service area and then a second group composed of individuals who sought healthcare within the hospital service area but were referred by a physician to a competing facility or those who sought a physician outside the service area. In addition, there should be an analysis of age trends that affect the population within the hospital's service area and also an analysis of the population trends over the past 10 years. Finally, there should be a market share analysis over the last five years. This analysis will track the hospital's market share growth or decline and also the market share growth or decline of major competing hospitals or outpatient facilities within the hospital's service area.

A Medical Staff Recruitment Plan will first of all assure the hospital that appropriate physicians are being recruited and placed. Second, such a plan will justify the recruitment of additional physicians, therefore deflecting much of the criticism that will be generated by the existing medical staff. Third, the recruitment plan will assist the hospital in identifying geographic areas in which additional physicians must be placed. Fourth, the recruitment plan will help identify specific centers of excellence and the physician specialty needed to meet the clinical goals of that center. Fifth, the plan will help fill in referral gaps, thereby reducing the number of patients who are referred to competing facilities or referred out of the service area. Sixth, physician recruitment will be a core service of a strategic medical staff relations plan.

Jackson and Coker, a recruiting firm, in a joint venture with Ernst and Young, publishes physician revenue studies. These studies provide national benchmarks for measuring physician activities and allow the hospital to measure the decline or growth of revenues and inpatient utilization of the physicians. In addition, each specialty can be measured as to its profitability for the hospital.

These national benchmarks provide an effective measure of the activity of the medical staff, specifically, whether or not based on these benchmarks, additional staff must be recruited. In the case of the national averages for average annual inpatient admissions/discharges, if a medical specialty is well above the national averages for inpatient admissions or discharges it indicates the possibility of the specialty being taxed beyond its resources because of too many patients seen by individual physicians or specialty. There is also the distinct possibility, because of over-utilization, that patients are being turned away because it may take a long time for appointments to be made or there may be too long a patient wait in the waiting room. The same case holds for the national benchmark known as the average annual revenue per admission.[1]

Another effective measure of physician activity and/or support of the hospital is utilizing the discharges by rank order and gross billings. By taking the total charges and expected revenues, this generates a percentage collectible rate. In calculating that, along with the number of discharges, one can generate an average gross margin per discharge for each physician. The same holds true for percentage of collectible charges. By taking the total charges generated by each physician and calculating the expected revenue, one can find a percent collectible rate. Divided by discharge, one can find an average gross margin per discharge. As an example, Dr. Jones has total charges of $248,479.00. The physician's expected revenue is $246,834.00. The physician's percent collectible is 99.34%. With 98 discharges, this provides the physician with a gross discharge margin of $2,518.71. This provides the hospital not only with recruitment information based on the number and kinds of specialty, but also generates the hospital information concerning the profitability of each of the physicians recruited.

Another important factor concerning the hospital in its recruiting efforts is competitive activities. This deals with the activities of

---

1. Jackson and Coker, Ernst and Young, *1991 Physician Revenue Study.*

hospitals, free-standing facilities and physicians that may affect the service level of the recruiting hospital. The best place to find out competitive information is to contact the local or state agencies that deal with a Certificate of Need (CON), or licensure of facilities and physicians. These agencies are usually able to provide up-to-date information concerning facility construction or the development of new technologies for competing facilities and/or physicians.

Another effective recruiting strategy is to track population growth and movement. This affords the hospital the ability to place physicians in rapidly growing suburban or urban areas. By contacting the county planning department, demographic and geographic information can be gained concerning population movement and demographic changes within the population. This will allow the hospital to place physicians geographically to tap specific growth areas and/or to place the appropriate specialty within population centers. Lastly, as a guide, each medical specialty projects the needs of its specific specialty based on an ideal physician/population ratio. By contacting each specialty board, this ideal physician population ratio can be acquired. Typically, though, the ideal physician population ratios are as follows:

Specialty	Population Served
Allergy	25,000 population
Anesthesiology	14,000 population
Family Practice	2,200 population
Cardiology	2,500 population
Dermatology	40,000 population
Gastroenterology	50,000 population
General Surgery	10,000 population
Internal Medicine	5,000 population
Neurology	60,000 population
Obstetrics/Gynecology	11,000 population
Ophthalmology	20,000 population
Pediatrics	10,000 population
Psychiatry	10,000 population

Urology   30,000 population
Otolaryngology   25,000 population

These ideal physician population ratios are a guide that will allow the hospital to project certain general patterns in physician recruitment. Other factors though, may be more important, such as demographic changes, population shifts, and certainly changes in reimbursement.

Chapter 3

Recruiting Agency versus In-House Recruiting Function

ADVANTAGES AND DISADVANTAGES

Should you use a recruiting agency or should you develop an in-house recruiting function? There are several advantages and disadvantages to both processes. By passing the responsibility onto a recruiting agency the administrator can save time, has access to an existing pool of physician candidates, and can enable the facility to buy time while it develops its own in-house recruiting function. Some of the disadvantages of using a recruiting agency are that the administration loses control over the recruiting process and the cost of recruiting may be increased. This last consideration, however, can be outweighed by the benefits of quickly recruiting a physician.

By developing an in-house function, the facility gains control over the recruiting process and becomes familiar with the physician candidate who is able to develop a trusting relationship with the recruiter and the administrator. Physician recruitment can also be the core activity for an active physician relations program.

The disadvantages are that it requires a Full-Time Equivalent employee and can be an expensive process. Physician recruiting can also be an overwhelming and time-consuming process and the individual responsible for physician recruiting can easily become burned out.

Usually, by the time a hospital starts recruiting, several things have happened. Either the board of trustees has told the administrator that there must be more physicians on staff to keep the hospital viable or a major hospital physician supporter has left, creating a gap in either the specialty or number of physicians on the medical staff. And the last issue may be that the hospital wishes to implement new services that call for specialty physicians and these specialty physicians must be recruited. Usually, the recruiting process is on-going; more than one physician must be recruited. Remember, too, that the recruiting process can be quite lengthy. The national average for recruiting a physician is over eight months. Usually, physicians have approximately five firm positions to choose from, so there is certainly no guarantee that you will recruit the physicians with whom you talk.

Therefore, a facility must decide whether to use a recruiting agency or develop an in-house recruiting function. One argument for having a recruiting agency is that by retaining or using a contingency recruiting firm, the administrator may save time by not having to recruit. This is only partially true. The recruiting agency is able to find, sometimes screen, and do a reference check on the physician, but it is up to the facility management to schedule site visits, to tour the physician through the facility and through the community, and to negotiate the contract. By using an agency, there is a ready-made, established pool of physician candidates and usually agencies have an extensive search network providing the hospital management immediate access to potential candidates.

An agency can also assist the facility in finding those hard-to-locate specialties. Search agencies have the resources to do mass mailings and general advertising, thereby increasing the chance of recruiting or providing to the hospital specialties that are difficult to find. Recruiting agencies also alleviate part of the responsibility from administration for recruiting, specifically, those front-end activities, such as prospecting for the physician, advertising, developing brochures and journal advertising. In addition, the agency can act as a search resource to facilities who are in the process of developing their own recruiting function. Using the agency as an interim physician recruiter while developing an in-house function can greatly facilitate the recruiting process for the facility. In addition, it is not unusual to find recruiting agencies who are willing to train and set up recruiting functions for the healthcare facility.

The disadvantages of using a recruiting agency are that it reduces the control over the physicians being recruited. The facility is subject to the physician candidates submitted by the recruiting agency. Usually the agency has done an initial reference check and feels the candidate may fit the needs of the hospital. Then again, especially in the case of a contingency recruiting agency, the agency may attempt to send as many résumés as possible in the hopes that the facility will pick one or more physicians to interview and ultimately hire.

Agencies are expensive. Typical range of contingency charges are between $18,000 and $25,000 per physician hired and specific, hard-to-find specialties are even more expensive. The issue of using a retained search firm or a contingency firm will be addressed in the section dealing with the recruiting process.

An advantage of the in-house recruiter is that there exists an intimate knowledge of the facility and the needs of the facility in the areas of physician recruitment. There is an awareness of the facility recruitment goals and efforts adhere to these goals since the recruiter has access to and meets often with the facility's management. By developing an in-house recruiting function an opportunity is provided for the recruiter to develop a trusting and productive relationship with the administrator. Remember, a positive recruiting relationship among those involved creates an atmosphere in which decisions can be made quickly to keep the recruiting process moving forward. This is vital to the success of a recruiting activity. If decision making is not facilitated the recruiting process bogs down and the physician perceives that there is little interest in his or her candidacy. In addition, competitors will act quickly to recruit potential candidates.

Physician recruiting can create a feeling in the recruiting administrator of being overwhelmed and discouraged. Most of the work is done over the telephone and in the evenings since that is the most effective time for reaching the physician candidate. And again, a good part of the recruiter's time will be spent in the evening, sometimes because of a physician's schedule, specifically for entertaining the candidate and his or her family. Much of the physician recruiting process also takes place on weekends.

CONCLUSIONS AND RECOMMENDATIONS

The most effective combination for providing you with a successful recruiting system is to use both a recruiting agency and an in-house recruiting function. By using both tools you will develop an immediate pool of physician candidates while providing ongoing support for the recruiting process and for enabling your recruiter to become expert in physician's relations activities. Once a recruiter places a physician it is necessary that the physician feels supported by the facility by receiving practice development services and/or marketing support for his or her practice. As in any organizational function it is essential that clear, concise recruitment criteria and goals be established. Only through a clear definition of the type of physician being recruited can resources be used effectively and efficiently.

WHO SHOULD DIRECT THE PHYSICIAN PROCESS?

The following is a job description of a Recruitment Director:

Job Identification

Job Title:	Director of Physician Services
Alternate Title:	Director of Medical Staff Support
Department:	Administration
Status:	Exempt
Grade:	N/A
Points:	N/A

Job Summary

Responsibilities include maintenance of current business and increase of the level of admissions from the *facility name* systems medical staff. The Director supports and manages the facility's physician recruitment efforts and provides practice support services for the medical staff. In addition, the Director manages the physician relations programs, including physician education and the speaker's bureau. The Director acts as the primary link between the management of the facility and its medical staff.

Major Responsibilities and Duties

1. Supports administration in its physician recruitment efforts.
2. Manages and coordinates the Physicians Speaker's Bureau.

3. Manages and coordinates the Physician Education Program.
4. Provides practice support and marketing services to newly recruited and established physicians.
5. Participates in negotiating recruitment contracts and leases.
6. Manages the operations of the Physician Recruitment Process.
7. Manages and coordinates the Physician Relations Program.
8. Works closely with facility departments to identify a physician's needs.
9. Monitors physician and hospital admission levels and takes corrective action when levels drop.

Remaining Responsibilities and Duties

1. Coordinates physician recruitment meetings.
2. Arranges Grand Rounds Programs.
3. Arranges meetings with physician recruits and vendors.
4. Personally contacts physicians and their office staff members.
5. Entertains physicians and their staffs when appropriate.
6. Attends medical staff meetings when appropriate.
7. Initiates and reviews strategic plans for changes in service levels.
8. Makes suggestions for new products and services based on information from physicians and office staff.
9. Handles physician practice problems as they arise.
10. Makes regular reports to administration concerning medical staff support services.
11. Monitors Physician Support Programs to ensure timeliness and success.
12. Monitors physician satisfaction levels, deals with physician complaints and works with administration to solve physician concerns.

Job Relationships

Reports to: Facility Chief Executive Officer

Supervises: Possibly an Assistant

Interrelationships: Administration, all facility department staffs, the medical staff, vendors, drug company representatives, and community organizers. Liaison with medical schools, residency programs, and physician search firms.

Equipment Instruments or Machines Used

1. Dictating machine, calculator, and computer.

Physical Demands and Working Conditions

1. Requires minimum physical effort.
2. Surroundings are pleasant.
3. Requires moderate amount of time spent in physician's office.
4. Requires some travel.
5. Requires evening and weekend work.

Minimum Job Requirements

1. Bachelor's Degree; prefer Master's Degree.
2. Working knowledge of healthcare, marketing, contracting, recruiting, and physician relations.
3. Program management skills.
4. Successful sales experience.
5. Negotiation, problem solving and customer relations skills.
6. Three to five years' experience.

Requested by: _____

Approved by: _____

Effective Date: _____

Revised: _____

Reviewed: _____

RESOURCE MATERIAL

Phase One: Prospecting for Physician Candidates

The following sources (alphabetically ordered) and basic procedures are proven methods for finding physicians for your facility.

1. *American Medical Association*

Obtain the AMA's *Physician Placement Register* that lists potential physician candidates. Request from the AMA the curriculum vitae (CV's) of selected candidates. The cost is $5.00 per curriculum vitae. Contact the physician that you want to consider further by mail and phone. Advertise any available positions in the *Journal of the American Medical Association.* In addition to the $5.00 per CV cost there is an additional charge for receiving the AMA listing on a monthly basis.

2. *Physician Search Firms*

As previously mentioned, search firms are a great help when just beginning and as a continuing source for specific physician specialties. But remember, physician recruiting agencies can be expensive to use. Fees for enlisting physician search firms can range from $18,000 to $25,000 or more per search.

3. *Pharmaceutical Companies*

An often overlooked source of potential physician candidates is pharmaceutical companies. Representatives from the companies have fairly intense contact with physicians throughout specific regions and usually have the inside information on physicians who may be willing to relocate. In addition, many pharmaceutical companies have a service that provides physicians a registry that allows physicians to search for new practice opportunities.

4. *Medical Boards*

Contact the medical board that represents the field of specialty for which you want to recruit. Virtually every specialty has its own board, usually listed in the American Hospital Association's *Guide to Healthcare Facilities.* Obtain the names of qualified physician candidates for a position, send a letter to each qualified physician candidate and follow up with a phone call.

5. *Military Programs*

Send a letter to the commanding officer of hospitals and establish a relationship with that person. Obtain a list of potential candidates for your position and send letters to those physicians. Create a file of military facilities and responses. Also, create a database for military facility information.

6. *Residency Programs*

This is probably the most fertile field for recruiting physicians. Send a letter to the school's residency coordinator (or Program Director), usually an individual who specifically controls the activities of the various residents. This is an extremely important individual with whom to become familiar and establish a personal relationship. An important source of information and potential referrals is the Chief Resident. This individual has intimate knowledge of those residents who are searching for positions, who have accepted positions or who are going on to a fellowship program. It is always a good idea to source residency programs one to two years before the residents graduate.

7. *Unsolicited Résumés*

Inevitably your facility will receive unsolicited resumes from physicians who are searching for a practice opportunity. Contact by mail and phone any qualified candidates whose résumés you have received.

8. *Word of Mouth*

Contact by mail and phone any qualified candidates whose availability has been made known to you. Existing medical staff are usually aware of residents or practicing physicians who are looking for a practice opportunity, so it is important to maintain a close working relationship with them.

Sample Letter to Physician Residency Coordinator

Date

Mr./Ms. Residency Coordinator
Graduate Medical Facility
P.O. Box 000
Residency Program, USA

Dear Mr./Ms. _____:

As we discussed over the telephone, (facility) is recruiting a

(list specialty) to establish a practice in (name of community).

Please distribute the attached bulletin to those residents who

are graduating during the current program. For further

information, please call me at (telephone number).

Sincerely,

Sample Letter to Physician Candidate

Date

John/Johanna Jones, MD
Department of (specialty)
P.O. Box 000
New York, New York

Dear Dr. Jones:

_____, a healthcare facility, located in
(community name) is seeking a (specialty) to establish a
private practice. (Facility name) offers the possibility of
linking new physicians with existing groups while providing
solo practice opportunities to physicians who would like to
locate in (name of community). A comprehensive recruitment
package is being offered that includes a guaranteed income,
office space, practice support services and a relocation
allowance.

The (name of facility) is located in (name of community) and
offers a complete array of cultural, social, and sports activities.
For further information, or to arrange a meeting, please call me
at (telephone number).

Sincerely,

Phase Two: Contacting and Selling the Physician Candidate

Use the following basic guidelines for contacting and influencing potential physician candidates.

Contacting Physicians

After a potential physician candidate has been identified, telephone the physician to make initial personal contact. Based on the telephone call and the interest of the physician and the facility, send a letter summarizing the points made in your telephone conversation and include information about the location and practice site opportunity that you are promoting. Send to the physician a complete recruitment packet, which should include:

- Information about your facility.
- Information about the area (usually this information is gathered by the Chamber of Commerce).
- Information about area banking.
- Information about the area's special characteristics and places of interest.
- Information about the school system (this is especially important if the physician has a family).
- A brief outline of the recruitment incentive package, including the name and telephone number of the contact person. It is important that a specific individual be identified as the contact person for the physician candidates. This reduces confusion and helps to build a bond between the recruiter and the physician candidate.

Determining Physician Candidate Availability

Through your contacts with the physician, try to determine the following information. By asking these critical questions, much time and possible expense will be saved:

- Has the physician found a position?
- Is the physician going on to a fellowship?
- Does the physician have an interest in the location?

- Does the opportunity you present meet the physician's needs?
- Will your incentive package attract the physician?
- What are the physician's practice objectives?

Obtaining Background Data on the Physician Candidate

Request that the physician send you a curriculum vitae and references. Although the references may not be contacted until later, it is always a good idea to have them because it saves time when indeed a reference check is necessary. At the time that references are necessary, contact each reference and create a database profile that includes the following information concerning the candidate:

- Address and telephone number
- Education
- Affiliations
- Special practice interests and/or qualifications
- Subjective data such as:
  possible substance abuse
  personal problems
  personality traits
  peer relations
- Keep complete notes on all conversations. If indeed you are keeping notes on a computer, make sure that the input is completed at the end of each telephone call. If you are using a manual system, keep on file complete notes of each conversation. It is always a good idea to list the dates of telephone and personal contact on the face of the physician candidate's folder. This keeps your memory fresh as to when other contacts must be made.

Arranging Site Visits

Once it has been determined that the physician candidate is appropriate to your opportunity, the next goal you face is scheduling a site visit. Many times this is the first time a personal contact is made between you and the physician. It is extremely important that the time within the site visit be used effectively. The physician should be kept busy but not overwhelmed. Free time should be provided during the day so that the physician and the physician's spouse, or significant other, can have an opportunity to discuss the practice opportunity. It is wise to schedule at least a day, and preferably a day and a half, for the visit so that the physician and his/her family can review your facility, the community, and the practice opportunity. For this visit you should:

- Make sure that the spouse (or significant other) makes the site visit with the physician. No physician will make a decision about moving to a practice site unless there is an opportunity to discuss it with the significant other. It is false economy to limit the site visit to the physician only. This will only extend the period of time the physician needs to make a decision and inevitably the significant other must see the practice location and the community before a decision can be made concerning a move. Remember, a good number of the decisions about moving to a new site are made by the spouse or significant other.
- Transport the physician and his/her family to and from the hotel and the facility.
- The first meeting should be a complete overview of the facility, its staff and its location.
- A meeting should be set up with the facility administrator, during which recruiting goals are discussed and an explanation is made concerning the need to recruit the candidate's specific specialty.
- Identify the areas of concern of both the physician and his/her spouse. Specifically, these areas of concern will include compensation, practice location and call coverage, which is extremely important. If indeed you will be recruiting a physician, make sure that some sort of call coverage is available. The last area of concern is practice support. What will the hospital do to make the practice successful?
- Give a general outline of the incentive package that you are offering.
- The recruiter's job is to help the physician begin a positive relationship with the facility administrator during this meeting.

- Arrange to have the designated relocation specialist meet with the physician's spouse or significant other to discuss relocation, tour the community, and observe its activities.
- Take the physician on a tour of the facility and introduce him or her to department staff.
- Have lunch with the physician, the facility administrator and a small group of the facility's physicians.
- Take the physician on a tour of the area and its other medical facilities.

Follow-up Activities

At the conclusion of the site visit, discuss with the physician his or her impressions, fears, any obstacles to relocating and any negative impressions the spouse or the physician may have. Other topics that should be discussed include:

- Incentive packages.
- Office space and office rent.
- Up-fitting costs are an extremely important area and could make the difference between recruiting a physician or not. Up-fitting costs are the charges for bringing the office site to the point of the physician's being able to open his/her practice. Usually there is an allowance for up-fitting costs but often the allowance covers only about half of the total up-fitting costs. Based on the remainder of the charges for up-fitting, a new physician may be looking at out-of-pocket costs ranging from $20,000 to $60,000. Very few, if any, new physicians are willing to accept that kind of financial burden. Care must be taken not to lose the physician because of the concern about up-fitting charges. The most effective way to address the issue of office up-fitting costs is simply to absorb the entire cost for the physician.
- Establish time frames for:
    follow-up contact
    providing and signing a contract
    relocation
    starting dates

Review Your Physician Candidate

Based on your data and impressions, review your desire to pursue the physician. Check with the staff members who met the physician to get their impressions, as well as the physicians who met the candidate. Meet with the facility administrator to review what the physician wants and develop strategies to pursue the physician based on the information revealed during the site visit.

Continue Pursuing the Candidate

If you decide to continue pursing the physician, send him or her a letter of intent that outlines your facility's goals, benefits and incentives. Request that the physician sign the letter of intent if he or she desires to join the facility's medical staff.

Follow up with a Telephone Call

The objective at this stage is to arrange a second site visit by the physician to sign the contract and to start developing the office site. Call the physician to determine whether he/she is still interested in your facility. Find out if the physician is satisfied with the incentive package, with relocating, with the timing of the office opening, or with other aspects of the opportunity.

If the physician is no longer interested in your offer, inquire about his/her possible interest in future opportunities and ask if he/she has colleagues that may be interested in your opportunity. If, on the other hand, the physician agrees to your offer, arrange a second site visit where you will:

- Present the recruitment contract for the physician to sign.
- Bring in the interior designer and construction crew to complete the planning for the physician's office.
- Acquaint the physician with the following vendors:
  - insurance carriers (malpractice and other)
  - bankers
  - telephone companies and telephone suppliers
  - office furniture supplier

–medical equipment salespersons
–leasing agents
–office operations consultants
–attorneys
–construction supervisor
–real estate agents
- Clear with the physician the office staff that will be needed to run the office and assist in staffing.

Physician's Visit: Discussion Topics

During the physician candidate's visit to your facility, the recruiter should ensure that the physician (and significant other) are introduced to the community, the facility, its campus and his/her potential associates. Additionally, the recruiter should review with the physician candidate the details of the financial agreement that have been proposed by the facility. It is wise to address the following areas when planning a physician site visit.

- Introduction to the community.
  –Business district
  –Business areas of professional interest to spouse/ significant other
  –Medical community and medical society leadership
  –Residential areas, schools and churches
  –Realtors to assist with housing
  –Architects and/or interior designers to assist with office planning
  –Other professional community participants
  –Chamber of Commerce to assist with community contacts
  –Social aspects such as civic clubs, country clubs, golf courses, etc.
- Introduction to the facility's buildings.
  –Hospital office buildings
  –Physician's offices and available space in other areas
  –Administrators to advise and assist with practice needs
  –Personnel department of facility to assist with office staffing
  –Facility heads of departments and their staff as resources for the new physician

- Details of the financial agreement.
  - –Incentives offered by the facility
  - –Incentives offered by the community
  - –Arrangements with physicians looking for an associate, specifically providing services for in-practice physicians to recruit colleagues
  - –Introduction to bankers through which personal loans and other financial help may be negotiated
  - –Introduction to attorneys and accountants from whom legal and business advice may be obtained

How to Involve Facility Administration

Your recruiting efforts will be more successful if you coordinate the activities of the individual who will assist in recruiting. Specifically, those department heads, personnel, and other hospital resources who will play either a major or minor role in the recruiting of a physician. Use the following as a guideline for organizing your efforts:

- It is essential that a recruiting committee be formulated. The recruiting committee should be made up of the appropriate management staff, representation from the board of directors or trustees, and also representation from in-house physicians, specifically, radiology, pathology or even emergency medicine. The recruitment committee is essential for the effective planning of the recruiting efforts. In addition, it will facilitate budgeting for the recruiting efforts and add legitimacy for the recruitment of additional physicians.

- The committee should meet once per month, or more often, until you have established your objectives, goals, budget and strategies. After goals have been established, the committee should meet on an as-needed basis to interview physicians, update progress, and participate in social events welcoming new physicians to the community.

- The physician recruiter is essential to the coordination of the recruiting efforts and communication back to the recruiting committee. The recruiter provides physician candidate information, an update on recruiting efforts, and submits reports to the recruiting committee concerning candidates and recruiting process. In addition, the recruiter organizes recruitment sources. The recruiter should be responsible for contacting potential recruitment resources, arranging the physician's site visits, and coordinating with either public relations or marketing concerning any advertisements for physician candidates. In addition, the recruiter should play a primary role in providing marketing and practice support services for the new physician.

- Working hand in hand with the physician recruiter is either the public relations director or the marketing director. These individuals help the recruiter coordinate marketing strategies to support the new physician in his or her practice. They develop, produce and distribute physician recruitment information packages and also develop and place advertisements to attract physician recruits to the facility. In addition, they work closely with the physician recruiter in providing practice support services for the new physician; specifically, developing brochures, placing ads, and assisting the new physician in meeting the public.

Chapter 4

Justification for Recruiting New Physicians

This chapter provides an outline for written justifications of physician recruitment. This justification should address the concerns of the medical staff about competitive issues and a basis for the recruiting of various specialties. Also provided are tables that identify the admissions and revenues generated by specific specialties.

PROPOSAL TO RECRUIT PHYSICIANS

To make your recruiting efforts more efficient and effective you will need to provide written justification to your facility's board and possibly even the medical staff for your recruitment efforts. An example of such a proposal follows and is an outline form that you may wish to follow.

Purpose

This recruitment document provides justification for the physician recruitment efforts at (facility name).

Objective

This recruitment document provides an analysis of the physician community that serves (facility name). It also ensures that appropriate physicians are being recruited and that there will be a financial benefit to the facility and community in relation to incentives that are offered to the physician candidate.

Strategy

Our strategy is for recruiting (specialty needed) specifically those specialties and sub-specialties that the facility needs. Our strategy will also provide an independent and supportive referring and referral network that is affiliated with (facility name).

Projected Needs

We calculated the physician-to-population ratios using the average of two sources.

1. Surviving and prospering in private practice.
2. Physician characteristics and distribution in the United States.

Based on these averages, the following physician population ratios are indicated for most specialties:

Specialty	Population to Support Physician
Allergy	22,000-26,000
Anesthesiology	16,000-21,000
Family Practice	1,700- 3,000
General Surgery	4,000- 6,000
Internal Medicine	2,000- 6,000
Neurology	40,000-80,000
Neuro-Surgery	60,000-80,000
Obstetrics/Gynecology	10,000-13,000
Ophthalmology	20,000-25,000
Orthopedics	25,000-30,000
Otolaryrngology	35,000-45,000
Pathology	19,000-25,000
Pediatrics	8,000-12,000
Plastic Surgery	40,000-60,000
Psychiatry	10,000-12,000
Radiology	14,000-17,000
Urology	30,000-40,000

Based on a service population of (enter facility service population) and using the above physician population ratios, the following physician numbers are needed for (facility name). To calculate the number of physicians needed simply divide the population needed to support a physician into the service area population. If, for example, the service area population is 100,000 that service area population will support one (1) Neuro-Surgeon or four (4) Orthopedic Surgeons or thirty (30) Family Practitioners and so on.

Physician population ratios provide a broad average for the recruitment of specific specialties. These figures act as base. Other statistics are necessary to refine the recruiting process and for effective goal development. The following are national statistics for admissions and revenue generated by specific physician specialties:

National Physician Statistics[1]
Average Number of Annual Admissions by Physician Specialty

Specialty	Average Annual In-Patient Admission
Obstetrics/Gynecology	155
General/Family Practice	114
Internal Medicine	113
Pediatrics	109
General Surgery	84
Hematology	76
Oncology	74
Pulmonary Disease	69
Cardiology	61
Orthopedic Surgery	56
Thoracic Surgery	56
Nuero-Surgery	53
Urology	51
Psychiatry	47
Gastroenterology	45

1. Jackson and Coker, Ernst and Young, 1991, *Physician Revenue Study.*

Cardiovascular Surgery	36
Necrology	36
Rheumatology	31
Plastic Surgery	22
Neurology	16
Otolaryrngology	14
Ophthalmology	6

To further assist in the refining of recruitment goals the following statistics provide the average annual in-patient revenue generated per physician.[2]

Specialty	Average Annual In-Patient Revenue
Internal Medicine	$603,000
General/Family Practice	$413,000
Obstetrics/Gynecology	$387,000
Pediatrics	$190,000
Pulmonary Disease	$608,000
Cardiovascular Surgery	$604,000
General Surgery	$572,000
Cardiology	$546,000
Neuro-Surgery	$525,000
Oncology	$525,000
Nephrology	$518,000
Orthopedic Surgery	$517,000
Hematology	$485,000
Psychiatry	$454,000
Thoracic Surgery	$421,000
Urology	$280,000
Gastroenterology	$275,000
Neurology	$159,000

---

2. Jackson and Coker, Ernst and Young, 1991, *Physician Revenue Study.*

Plastic Surgery	$149,000
Rheumatology	$149,000
Otolaryrngology	$114,000
Ophthalmology	$ 39,000

A recent nationwide study indicated that four of the five highest paid facility admitters were primary care physicians. The average yearly facility admissions for the following specialties are:[3]

Family Practice	114
General/Internal Medicine	113
Obstetrics/Gynecology	155
Pediatrics	109

The average yearly revenue generated by physicians per admission per year is:

Internal Medicine	$603,000
General/Family Practice	$413,000
Obstetrics/Gynecology	$387,000
Pediatrics	$190,000

Specialty physicians generate the following in-patient revenue:

Pulmonary Disease	$608,000
Cardiovascular Surgery	$604,000
General Surgery	$572,000
Cardiology	$546,000
Neuro-Surgery	$525,000
Oncology	$525,000
Necrology	$518,000
Orthopedic Surgery	$517,000
Hematology	$485,000
Psychiatry	$454,000

---

3. The tables on this page are from: Jackson and Coker, Ernst and Young, 1991, *Physician Revenue Study.*

Thoracic Surgery	$421,000
Urology	$280,000
Gastroenterology	$275,000
Neurology	$159,000
Plastic Surgery	$149,000
Rheumatology	$149,000
Otolaryrngology	$114,000
Ophthalmology	$ 39,000

Again, for your planning purposes, a combination of the various statistics should be calculated. Based on the national averages for facility admissions and on the revenues generated by the various physician specialties, if we attain the recruitment goals specified, the (facility name) stands to gain the following, as an example:[4]

Specialty	National Average Admissions	Facility Recruitment Goal	Increase
Obstetrics/ Gynecology	155	2	310
General & Internal Medicine	113	6	678
Family Practice	114	4	456
Pediatrics	109	4	436

Such average admissions increases can be calculated based on the statistics that were given in the previous columns designating average annual in-patient admissions.

The same calculations can be made concerning additional revenues. Not measured are the additional admissions and revenues to the healthcare facility generated through out-patient services.

COMPETITIVE ACTIVITY

Offering physician recruitment incentives is not new in the healthcare field. Literature that discusses physician recruitment de-

---

4. Jackson and Coker, Ernst and Young, 1991, *Physician Revenue Study.*

scribes financial incentives, such as guaranteed income, as "an investment in the future." Harry E. Olson, MD, in his book *Physician Recruitment In The Hospital*, describes financial incentives as a "feature of many recruitment programs." Other incentives suggested by Dr. Olson are office rent subsidies, low interest loans, and assistance with purchasing office furniture and medical equipment.

Financial incentives are necessary to recruit physicians. There is no other way to get around it. Without some way of providing financial incentives to help the physician overcome initial cash flow difficulties, recruitment becomes more difficult, if not impossible. "The key to successful recruiting is gaining consensus on the type and priority of physicians desired and developing a sound financial package."[5]

Most physician candidates need some type of financial start-up support to assist with equipment purchases, operating expenses, and cash flow. They need, and can usually find, income guarantees to support self and family. The physician recruit must feel that your facility is able to offer competitive financial support. A competitive package is a major influence in the physician candidate's selection of a location.

Physicians have at least five firm opportunities besides yours to choose from. While interviewing physician candidates, it must be remembered that other area facilities are offering competitive financial recruitment packages which are quite comprehensive and often include some of the following:

- Interview Expenses
- Guaranteed Income
- Moving Expenses
- Medical Office Rental Assistance
- Low Interest Loans
- Payment or Assistance in Malpractice Insurance Costs
- Subsidizing the Cost of Medical Practice Consulting and Medical Practice Marketing
- Subsidy of Employees' Salaries

---

5. The Saslaw Group, *Medical Staff Marketing Advisory,* Volume 1, Number 1, July 1987.

- Office personnel hiring expenses paid, especially when a staffing firm is used

A recent survey of 114 hospitals found that almost all are recruiting physicians. As an incentive, the hospitals are offering physicians guaranteed incomes of between $75,000 and $180,000 annually, depending on specialty. The surveyed hospitals are offering other incentives, including moving expenses, assistance with recruiting staff, and marketing support.

A separate study found that 58% of U.S. hospitals are recruiting physicians. Recruitment is necessary because there is a shortage of family practitioners, general internists, obstetricians/gynecologists, orthopedic surgeons and other specialties. Almost half the surveyed hospitals are offering free office rent in hospital-owned medical office buildings. It is an unusual facility that does not need to recruit physicians. One key to developing a successful recruiting function is to provide recruitment incentives. Remember that the average annual inpatient revenue per physician is $550,000. It is likely that the recruiting package that you provide for the physician candidate will be paid pack within one year. Typically, a physician breaks even between three and six months of practice, meaning that the incentive package that you offer to a physician candidate is a cost at very low risk and may not be a cost at all. In summary, physician recruitment is necessary to keep the healthcare facility competitive. Physician recruitment will increase utilization, strengthen revenues, and service the public more effectively.

GUIDELINES FOR EFFECTIVE RECRUITMENT PLANS

To recruit effectively you first need an effective recruitment plan. This chapter will deal with a detailed summary of the plan that is given to you in Chapter 1. This plan is a written compilation of all the elements of your recruiting efforts. Use the plan to inform administration and physicians of your intent and as a tool to guide and coordinate your recruitment activities, both present and future. A recruitment plan comprises three main elements: an executive summary; the recruitment plan; and supporting documentation. These elements are described below.

Executive Summary

The executive summary is a general outline of your recruitment plan to let you and others review your recruiting purpose goals and procedures without reading the entire document.

Recruitment Plan

There are many points to consider in preparing your formal recruitment plan. Before you begin your written plan, review these aspects of your plan and make note of how they may affect your plan.

First introduce your plan. State your purpose clearly then detail your recruitment plan. Consider the following:

Evaluate Your Need

Determine how many physicians you need at your facility and in what specialties and for what geographic area your facility serves. Determine which of these needs are primary and which are secondary.

Survey the Population

Select a random sample of your market population to determine the need for additional physicians and services. From this survey also determine the impact that more physicians will have on your facility and community then identify your needs and establish your priorities. You will want to use this information to solicit support.

Form a Recruitment Committee

Form a committee of persons that will assist you in recruiting physicians. Identify the purpose of this committee and what resources you will use to recruit physicians. This committee should include a designated chairperson, administrators, medical staff members, board members, and the recruiter.

Plan Committee Activities

The recruitment committee reviews planning data, assigns specific responsibilities, plans promotions, identifies sources of physicians, assesses community and area resources, and needs, prepares community profiles, and begins interview and visit planning.

Begin the Recruitment Process

The recruiter develops contacts and prospects' lists, determines contact responsibility and verifies credentials. In addition, he or she conducts interviews, conducts site visits, evaluates site visits, formulates incentives, and assists in negotiation and issuance of contract agreements.

Help Set up Practice

When the physician has been successfully recruited, the recruiter assists with setting up the physician's new practice. The recruiter refers the physician to the proper resources for furniture, equipment and supplies, and assists with hiring personnel. The recruiter also publicly announces the new office opening through the use of newspaper, media, advertising, and direct mail.

Retain the New Recruit

To ensure that the recruited physician stays at the facility and remains satisfied, the recruiter assists the physician with any adjustment problems. The recruiter evaluates the physician's professional needs and meets them or offers a referral source. Additionally, the recruiter monitors the facility's personnel response to the new physician and uses this information to direct retention efforts.

Evaluate Your Strategies

When the physician has successfully established his/her practice, the recruiter then reviews the recruitment process on a case-by-case basis and evaluates its strengths and weaknesses. The recruiter then modifies the recruitment plans to make improvements and meet projected needs.

Supporting Documentation

Include a reference list with your plan that cites the names of all sources of information you used to support your plan. Attach additional pages of copies or formulated information that provides evidence of your claims. The following is an outline of a recruitment plan:

Purpose of the Plan

Help practicing physicians to recruit other physicians to share call and overhead and to expand the practice services area and gain market share.

Provide retiring physicians with the opportunity to sell or transfer their practices to younger physicians.

Recruit physicians to fill a need based on specialty and geographic location.

Recruit physicians to fill a need based on service line development and additional technology.

RECRUITMENT PLAN

I. Plan the recruitment process
  A. Designate a recruitment committee comprising
    1. Appropriate administration
    2. Board Members
    3. Physician recruiter
    4. Appropriate physicians
  B. Make the recruitment committee responsible for determining:
    1. Number of physicians to be recruited
    2. Specialties to be recruited
    3. Geographic areas to place physicians
    4. Criteria for assisting physicians in recruiting a colleague
    5. Budget
  C. Create an inducement package

II. Use sources of physician recruits
   A. Military bases
   B. Local and national residency programs (obtain recruits from list of residents sent from the residency program)
   C. Media promotions such as recruiting ads in medical publications
   D. Federal programs
   E. Physicians wanting to recruit colleagues
   F. Physician search firms
   G. Specialty seminars or conventions where potential recruits gather

III. Access the Physician Recruit
   A. Review curriculum vitae
      1. Call medical schools
      2. Contact references
      3. Match criteria with specialty needs
      4. Conduct a site visit and interview
   B. Send the physician candidate an information package that includes:
      1. message of welcome from the C.E.O.
      2. facility annual report
      3. description of facility buildings and capabilities
      4. map of the local area
      5. description of the city
      6. recent Sunday newspapers
      7. description of recreational facilities
      8. real estate report and sample home prices
      9. description of shopping centers and retail stores
      10. economic statistics of the area
      11. geographic relationships to other cities
      12. climate conditions
      13. description of educational facilities
      14. description of cultural activities
      15. description of recreational activities
   C. Plan the physician's visit
      1. Have the physician pay for his own travel but reimburse the physician at the time of his arrival. If the travel is pre-

paid, there is the opportunity for the physician to back out. If the physician pays on his or her credit card, there is more incentive for the physician to keep the site visit date.

2. Invite the physician's spouse or significant other. No physician will make a decision to move to a specific area without input from spouse or significant other. It is a strategic mistake not to invite the physician's spouse. This will be costly in the long run. If the spouse is not happy with the location, no further expenses need be spent on this physician. But if the physician's spouse or significant other likes the location and expresses a willingness to move, then the recruiting process needs to proceed.

3. Meet the physician and spouse to go over their schedule. That includes:
   a. a tour of the facility
   b. a tour of the city
   c. meeting with the administration and selected physicians

4. Follow up after the physician's visit
   a. with a phone call
   b. if the recruiting committee is interested, send a letter of intent to the candidate
   c. use an employment firm; find employment for the physician's spouse
   d. look for potential practice sites
   e. discuss the inducement package with the physician
   f. contact banks for credit lines

D. Develop the incentive package* which may include:
   1. total or partial office rent subsidy for a specific period of time
   2. salary guarantee
   3. transferable life insurance
   4. moving expenses
   5. guaranteed low interest loans

---

*All elements of the incentive package should be defined and approved before recruiting efforts begin.

      6. guaranteed credit lines
      7. marketing assistance
      8. financial grant for office equipment
      9. office staff hiring assistance
    10. emergency or urgent care work to supplement income
    11. practice announcements for the new physician

E. Retain the new physician
    1. assist the new physician in establishing a referral network
    2. help the physician's spouse to assimilate into the community
    3. help the physician's spouse find employment
    4. assist the physician in gaining hospital privileges
    5. provide marketing support with speaker bureau, promotions, and physician referral support

Chapter 5

Contracts

Contracts play an essential role in the recruitment of physicians. Contracts are the basis for developing and providing incentives and practice support activities for the physician. Contracts clearly set down the responsibilities of both the facility and the physician and the contract also is a primary form of protection for the recruiting facility concerning the issues of "Safe Harbors," "Stark Legislation" and "General Council Memorandum."

Before any consideration can be made concerning contractual arrangements with a physician candidate, the facility's attorney must review any contracts or written agreements with the physician candidate. This is necessary because of Stark Anti-Referral Legislation. The Stark Bill was passed in December of 1989 as part of the Omnibus Budget Reconciliation Act (OBRA) of 1989, becoming section 1877 of the Social Security Act, titled *Limitations on Certain Physician Referrals*. As a general prohibition, effective January 1, 1992, a physician may not make prohibited referral to a clinical laboratory and a clinical laboratory may not present a claim to Medicare or Medicaid or bill any individual, third-party payor or any entity for clinical laboratory services furnished pursuant to a prohibited referral. A prohibited referral is considered any referral to an entity in which the physician or an immediate family member has a financial relationship.[1]

Not only does the Stark Legislation affect referrals, but it affects all elements of a physician recruitment incentive package. As of 1990, there were certain exceptions to compensation arrangements

---

1. The National Health Lawyers' Association, 1990 Health Law update and annual meeting.

for recruiting physicians known as "safe harbors." The first exception is the rental of office space for a physician candidate. When rental office space is provided for a physician candidate, there must be a written lease, the term must be of at least one year, the rent must be consistent with fair market value that does not vary based on volume or value of referrals and the rent must be considered commercially reasonable, even in the absence of referrals. The office space must be in the same building as the physician's practice is located, or in the group practice, and the arrangement must meet such other arrangements as Secretary of Health and Human Services may impose on regulation to protect against programs or patient abuse.

Any other sections of the recruitment agreement must have specific language that prohibits Medicare and Medicaid referrals to a hospital based on a benefit that inures to the physician. In general, the Stark Legislation provides safe harbors when "the amount of remuneration is consistent with fair market value and not determined in relation to volume or value of referrals."[2]

Unfortunately, Stark Legislation and Safe Harbors seems to be rather fluid with changes taking place within the legislation on a fairly regular basis. Therefore, it is imperative that your incentive recruitment package be reviewed by your attorney specific to compliance with Safe Harbors Legislation.

The following pages contain various forms and contracts used in physician recruitment. Again, it is imperative that these forms be reviewed by your attorney prior to any recruiting activities.

---

2. Ibid., National Health Lawyers' Association.

RESIDENCY PROGRAM SPECIALTY

Chairman: _____

Program Name: _____

Address: _____

_____

_____

_____

Phone Numbers: _____

_____

_____

Chief Resident: _____

Notes: _____

_____

_____

_____

_____

_____

_____

MILITARY HEALTHCARE FACILITIES SPECIALTY

Military Base: _____

Contact Person: _____

Title: _____

Address: _____

_____

_____

_____

Phone Numbers: _____

_____

_____

Notes: _____

_____

_____

_____

_____

_____

_____

_____

_____

RECRUITMENT SOURCES

Organization: _____

Contact Person: _____

Address: _____

_____

_____

_____

Phone Numbers: _____

_____

_____

Specialty: _____

_____

_____

_____

Costs: _____

_____

VENDOR CONTACTS

Name: _____

Company: _____

Address: _____

_____

_____

_____

Phone Numbers: _____

_____

_____

Product/Service: _____

_____

_____

_____

_____

_____

_____

_____

Chapter 6

Incentives

Recruitment incentives are an accepted practice within healthcare. Caution must be exercised when recruiting due to the current issues concerning Medicare/Medicaid fraud and abuse laws, Stark, and General Council Memoranda (GCM).

Incentives are discussed in this chapter and typical recruitment incentive packages are detailed.

The following are incentives offered by hospitals throughout the U.S.

1. Free office space for a specified period of time subject to Safe Harbors Legislation.
2. Loan of office equipment with option for physician to purchase.
3. Salary of personnel for one year.
4. Free accountant services to assist with business matters of the practice.
5. Assistance with hiring personnel.
6. Free housing for a specified period of time.
7. Low interest loans for office equipment and housing.
8. Paid moving expenses.
9. Guaranteed income.
10. A relocation grant.

The following are two examples of recruitment packages that could be offered to physicians.

Example 1:

1. Rental Assistance
   A. Rental free for one year with no pay backs.
   B. Office set up.

2. Financial Assistance
   A. Guaranteed gross incomes based on specialty, as an example: $10,000 per month guaranteed for a urologist, $8,000 per month guaranteed for a general surgeon.
   B. Interview expenses paid for both the physician and significant other.
   C. Repayment loans can be in service at the rate of $\frac{1}{36}$ of the loan amount per month. The physician also has the option of paying back loans at $2,000 per month. If the physician maintains the payment level, the loan stays interest free.
   D. Facility may pay malpractice insurance for the first year.
   E. Facility may pay off all student loans and/or grants.

3. Personnel Assistance
   A. Screen résumés for physician's office staff.
   B. Set up physician's telephone system one month before physician starts practicing. The administrative offices or the physician referral service answer the telephone providing the physician with appointments on the day the office opens.

4. Promotional Assistance
   A. Place newspaper announcements for the opening of the physician's office.
   B. Provide the physician business cards.
   C. Place the physician on the hospital speaker's bureau.
   D. Provide marketing planning and marketing support for the new physician.
   E. Assist the physician in developing referral lines and support.

Example 2:

1. Rental Assistance
   A. Free office rent for one year.

2. Financial Assistance
   A. Household moving expenses paid with a cap.
   B. Interview expenses paid for physician and spouse or significant other.
   C. Home loan guarantee.
   D. Interest free loans.
   E. Income guarantee.
   F. Offer group purchase program by vendors.

3. Personnel Assistance
   A. Business office management consultants provided.

4. Practice Support Program
   A. Facilities provide assistance in:
      1. Collecting demographic information.
      2. Planning practice marketing strategies.
      3. Promoting practice through the media.

GENERAL COUNCIL MEMORANDUM: EXPLANATION

The following is a letter from an attorney to a healthcare facility that outlines the general counsel memorandum concerning physician recruitment incentive packages.

The purpose of this letter is to outline the procedures and guidelines regarding physician recruitment. As was discussed, the Internal Revenue Service recently issued a general counsel memorandum (GCM 39498) that addresses this area.

The overall focus of the GCM is that of ensuring that the hospital provide a compensation package to the recruited physician that is reasonable in total. Therefore, it is important to quantify the maximum amount that can be received by the physician (including relocation costs and non-cash incentives, such as free use of space) under the program.

Since the basic test is that of "reasonableness of total compensation paid," each contract should be individually reviewed and negotiated. It is unlikely that all physicians should command the same total package. Rather, specialization, experience level, etc., should be separately considered. Documentation of the process then becomes a critical factor.

Specifically, the total compensation package should be reviewed by the board of directors and expressly approved (as documented in the minutes) citing that the total level is reasonable for such consideration as:

- The difficulty in recruiting physicians to the specific location.
- How much neighboring hospitals pay physicians with similar backgrounds.
- The service to be directly performed by the physician for the hospital.
- The need for the particular physician specialty in the community.

The IRS has indicated that a minimum income guarantee will not jeopardize the hospital's 501(c)3 exempt status provided that subsidies made pursuant to a guarantee must be paid with fair market interest at some future time. In those cases where repayment provision is not included (since it substantially reduces the hospital's ability to negotiate with the perspective physicians), the answer is somewhat unclear. However, certain other provisions in the contract can minimize concerns. Specifically, if an unconditional payback is not negotiable, the amount of modified payback requirements should be considered. This would convert into loans at fair market interest rates and any subsidies paid should the physician discontinue his or her medical practice in the area during the designated time period following the subsidy period. An even better solution is to initially record subsidies as loans with an earn-out provision. For example, assume there is a two-year contract that provides for a guaranteed income of $60,000 per year and that the hospital advances $5,000 in year one and $4,000 in year two. The contract could provide that the $9,000 advance represents loans subject to repayment, however, and that the total due is to be reduced by 25% for each year that the physician maintains a local practice after the final contract year. Thus, the physician has no payback if he or she maintains the practice for four subsequent years. Presumably, the compensation element (for purposes of determining the reasonableness of the package) would likewise be limited in years one and two since the advances are in the form of loans. Of course at the time of the earn-out, the amounts would be included in the total package for those years to determine the reasonableness at that time.

A ceiling on the amount of subsidy should also be clearly specified. In the GCM, the IRS indicated that it is important that the hospital determine the reasonableness of the overall compensation package in advance. This is difficult if no subsidy ceiling is imposed. For example, if the contract provides for a guarantee of $60,000 per year the hospital could pay $0.00-$60,000 if the practice makes money, $60,000 if the practice breaks even or more than $60,000 if the practice does poorly. Therefore, an overall ceiling on the subsidy should be stated. Based on directives it appears that when a ceiling is imposed then the guarantee is based on collections rather than net income. However, a definite statement regarding the maximum to be paid is suggested. This ceiling amount should then be used when evaluating the reasonableness of the overall package. Should it become necessary to make advances in excess of the stated ceiling, additional amounts could be made as loans that must be repaid (not subject to earn-out) with interest.

The IRS has recognized that hospitals can offer a one-time recruitment bonus based upon the value of the physician (looking to specialty, experience, etc.) rather than direct services to be provided. If such a bonus is offered, it must also be considered as part of an overall package to the physician. If no bonus is contemplated, the hospital may focus on some portion of the income guarantee as a substitute for the up-front bonus. The hospital might determine it is better to give a small one-time bonus with a more generous income guarantee expecting that payment will be minimal under the subsidy arrangement. The business decision process that weighs the timing and total of expected cash outlays (under each of the two options) should be fully documented.

Finally, all recruitment arrangements should be reviewed with legal counsel with compliance with the various Medicare/Medicaid fraud and abuse provisions.[1]

---

1. Robert Wilson, Attorney; Maupin, Taylor, Ellis, and Adams; Raleigh, North Carolina.

SAMPLE LETTER OF INTENT

Dear Doctor _____:

Based on our mutual interest in having you establish a private (specialty) practice at (facility name) this practice support proposal outline is being submitted to you. The goals of this proposal are to:

- Provide your practice a mechanism to reduce risk associated with establishing a new practice.
- Assist you in obtaining an income level consistent with a private (specialty) practice.
- Assist you in becoming a full-time private (specialty) in (city name).
- Make available to (facility name) comprehensive (specialty) services.
- Help you establish a (specialty) care inpatient services.
- Assist you in capturing market share in your practice service area.
  This letter of intent will be the basis of a contractual agreement between your practice and (facility name).

The subsequent contractual agreement will be structured to meet the above-mentioned goals and provide your practice:

- Cash flow to meet operational expenses.
- Salary.
- Practice management and practice support services.
- Relocation of your household to (city and state).

The following is our proposal:

- A one year collections guarantee in the amount of ($$$.000).
- Office space at no cost (location) for _____ years.
- Absorption of all up-fitting costs for your office.
- Payment of interest on a (amount) dollar loan for _____ year not to exceed _____%.

Page 1

- Office management consultation for _____ years not to exceed _____ dollars.
- Practice marketing support for _____ months, _____ hours per week valued at a total of _____ dollars.
- Moving allowances not to exceed _____ dollars.

Please contact me at (telephone number) should you have any questions. If you are in agreement with this proposal, please sign and date before (closing date).

Sincerely,

_____

Doctor's Signature:_____

Date:_____

Chapter 7

Legal Issues

To maintain the integrity of the non-profit hospital's 501(c)(3) status and for any hospital to ensure its Medicare/Medicaid status facilities must be sensitive to legal and regulatory recruitment limitations.

These recruitment limitations are found in "Stark Legislation," "Safe Harbors Regulations" and Internal Revenue Service "General Council Memorandum." Each of these restrictions is described in this chapter and their effects on the hospitals' incentives to recruit physicians. This chapter attempts to make you aware of consequences of these regulations and encourages you to seek legal advice when contracting with physicians.

Based on the concern about the provisions of the Stark Amendment, Safe Harbors, and the issue of inurement concerning the hospital's 501(c)3 designation as a nonprofit organization, the following memorandum will help the recruiter and the facility's administration in better defining the physician income guarantee agreement.

MEMORANDUM DEFINING PHYSICIAN INCOME GUARANTEE AGREEMENTS

The purpose of this memorandum is to discuss and make recommendations concerning specific aspects of the proposed physician income guarantee agreement (the agreement). First, must be considered the requirements imposed by (the facility's) tax exempt status, including the prohibition against any private inurement of the hospital's assets to another party such as a physician. In addition, we consider the Medicare and Medicaid fraud and abuse provisions, codified as 42USC Section 1395nn, and 1396h that prohibits the facility from giving any economic benefit to a physician in exchange for referral of Medicare or Medicaid patients to the facility. Given the developing nature of law in these areas, the risk to (the facility) inherent in the agreement cannot be entirely eliminated. However, we have several recommendations to assist you in structuring this agreement in order to minimize the risk to (the facility).

PRIVATE INUREMENT ISSUE

Under Internal Revenue Code Section 501(c)3, a tax-exempt hospital must be organized and operated for the charitable purpose of providing healthcare. In addition, it must be operated to serve public rather than private interest and no part of the hospital's earnings may inure to the benefit of private parties. Even a minimal amount of private inurement could result in the loss of the hospital's tax-exempt status.

The issue of private inurement must be considered in any contract for recruitment of a physician to a facility because the facility is proposing to transfer some of its resources to a physician as an inducement in recruiting the physician. The Internal Revenue Service (IRS) will look at all of the facts and circumstances of a particular arrangement in determining whether the arrangement is commercially reasonable and whether the guarantee or other considerations is necessary to the tax-exempt purpose of the hospital.

On April 24, 1986, the IRS issued a general counsel memorandum (GCM) in which the general counsel of the IRS concluded that a healthcare facility's proposed contract for a guaranteed minimum annual income, as part of its physician recruitment program, may result in private inurement and provide a basis for rescinding that facility's tax-exempt status. The IRS general counsel indicated that the determination of private inurement must be based on the specific facts and circumstances of the arrangement and refused to give advance approval to the proposal. Under such circumstances the facility must be very cautious to assure that the consideration paid to the physician is reasonable in relation to the benefit to the facility and is necessary to the facility's tax-exempt purpose.

There are several steps that the facility can take in order to minimize the risk of a finding of private inurement in its physician recruitment program. First, the facility should prepare a *written business analysis* (authors' italics) of the proposed arrangement in order to assure that the financial benefits to the facility will reasonably compensate the facility for its payments to or for the physician. The facility may conclude that the new physician would increase the facility's revenues by permitting the facility to offer services in a new specialty. Similarly, a quantitative business analysis may indicate that recruitment of a new physician will increase the facility's inpatient days, ancillary procedures or outpatient visits; however, as discussed below the financial benefit to the hospital should not be predicated on a promise of referrals of Medicare or Medicaid patients from the physician to the hospital because that could violate the above-referenced fraud and abuse provisions.

In addition to preparing a written business analysis, the facility may be able to demonstrate the commercial reasonableness of its proposal by reference to comparable recruitment packages for similar types of physicians. If any facility seeking to recruit a physician in a particular specialty would be required to provide certain incentives, that fact may assist in demonstrating the reasonableness of the arrangement. However, any comparison with other recruitment packages should be based on existing knowledge of the field or on published data and there should be no exchange of salary or benefit information with any competitors because that could result in possible violation of anti-trust laws.

Finally, a *written business analysis* should indicate the ways in which recruitment of a particular physician is necessary to advance the facility's tax-exempt purpose. For example, the hospital's primary purpose of providing healthcare would be advanced by expanding the facility services into a new specialty area or by improving the quality of care for existing services. If the facility carefully analyzes the documents, the commercial reasonableness, and necessity of each proposed contract will minimize the risk of a finding of private inurement.

MEDICARE AND MEDICAID FRAUD AND ABUSE

Federal law prohibits giving or receiving any payment in exchange for referral of a patient whose care will be paid for by the

Medicare or Medicaid programs C42USC, Sections 1395nn and 1396h. There are criminal as well as civil penalties for the prohibited activities and the potential for exclusion from participation in those programs. The Medicare and Medicaid Patient Program Protection Act of 1987, enacted in August 1987, consolidates the existing criminal penalty provisions for Medicare and Medicaid and extends their application to the maternal and child health block grant and the social services block grant programs. It also increases some criminal penalties. The act further provides that the Secretary of Health and Human Services, with the Attorney General, will issue regulations specifying payment practices that shall not be treated as criminal offenses and shall not service as bases for exclusion from the Medicare and Medicaid programs (public law 100-93,101 STAT 680,697). However, payment practices to be specified in these regulations will merely establish additional "Safe Harbors" and will not impose additional prohibition. At this time no final regulations have been issued.

In addition to obviously illegal activities, such as kickbacks, the language of the federal statute prohibits other financial arrangements between facilities and physicians that are designed to increase referrals of Medicare or Medicaid patients, CEG *United States vs. Greber, 760F.2d 68(1985)*. In *Greber* a federal court of appeals held that it is unlawful to pay a physician to induce him or her to use the payors' services "even if the payments were also intended to compensate for professional services."

Although the language of the statute and the *Greber* decision would appear to outlaw almost all financial arrangements between a facility and its referring physicians, most commentators predict that the statute will be interpreted in a reasonable manner. Nevertheless, the facility should structure the contract in question so as to minimize any risk of challenge on these grounds.

There is no evidence that the facility intends to compensate a physician directly or indirectly in exchange for referral or Medicare or Medicaid patients to that facility. However, if the contract requires the physician to spend a minimum number of hours or a certain percentage of his time at the facility, there is some risk that the contract could be challenged as an indirect method of obtaining referrals of Medicare or Medicaid patients to that facility. Therefore, it is recommended to delete any language that obligates the physician to utilize the facility's services for a minimum number of hours per week.

If business considerations dictate that the agreement contains some explicit obligation on the physician's part to utilize the services of the facility, it is recommended that the physician agree to use the facilities for the care of non-Medicare and non-Medicaid patients for whom hospitalization or treatment at the facility would be medically appropriate. Furthermore, the contract should explicitly state that the physician has no obligation to refer Medicare or Medicaid patients to the facility but has the options of utilizing its facilities for such patients.

A suggested paragraph has been prepared containing suggested language appropriate to this memorandum. In addition, all conforming changes should be made to the contract in order to delete any obligation on the part of the physician to use the facility for a minimum number of hours per week or a minimum percentage of his or her time.

To further support the legitimate purpose of the benefits provided, the agreement should specify any services that the physician is required to perform for the hospital, such as acting as director of a department or officer of the medical staff. However, the facility should not compensate a physician for such services in an amount that exceeds the fair market value of those services because that could lead to a charge that the compensation for services is an indirect method of compensation for referrals of Medicare or Medicaid patients.

SUGGESTED LANGUAGE TO PROTECT AGAINST MEDICARE, MEDICAID FRAUD AND ABUSE

The parties recognize that it would be unlawful for a facility to compensate a physician for a referral of Medicare or Medicaid patients to the facility and it is the intent of the parties that no compensation or remuneration of any kind whatsoever be paid under the agreement for referral of Medicare or Medicaid patients. However, in consideration of the benefits made available to the physician by the facility hereunder at all times during the effectiveness of this agreement and for a period of two years thereafter, the physician agrees to utilize the services of the facility for the inpatient and outpatient diagnosis and treatment of all of the facility's non-Medicare and non-Medicaid patients for whom, in the physician's professional judgment, such facilities are medically appropriate. The physician shall have no obligation whatsoever to utilize the facilities of the hospital for his or her Medicare or Medicaid patients but he or she shall have the option to utilize those facilities for such patients if he or she so desires. The physician also agrees to establish a physician call schedule for providing after-hours and weekend care for emergency and non-emergency patients requiring admission, inpatient follow-up care, outpatient and emergency care and observation services provided by the facility.

The following pages contain two sample contracts. These contracts have been used in an actual recruiting situation, but, remember due to the fluidity of Medicare and Medicaid Fraud and Abuse laws and the Stark Safe Harbors, be sure to have the contracts reviewed by an attorney.[1]

---

1. Robert Wilson, attorney; Maupin, Taylor, Ellis, and Adams; Raleigh, North Carolina.

PHYSICIAN INCOME GUARANTEE AGREEMENT

This agreement is entered into this _____ day of_____,

199__ by and between _____ (hospital)

and _____ , MD (physician).

1. **Recitals**
   a. The hospital is the owner of a ____ bed medical surgical hospital located in _____ (county) _____ state and the provider of hospitalization services for the medical/surgical patients.
   b. The physician is a _____ (specialty) and is eligible for licensure in the state of_____ and intends to establish a private practice in the _____ (county), _____ (state).
   c. The parties wish to establish a continuing relationship as hereinafter provided.

1. *Obligations of Doctor*
   a. On or before _____ the physician shall establish a private practice (hereinafter referred to as the "practice") in close proximity to the hospital. Throughout the term of this agreement, the physician shall in good faith and with diligence pursue his/her practice on a full-time basis. The physician shall maintain regular office hours for a minimum of 40 hours per week, 50 weeks per year.
   b. If the physician is not already licensed to practice _____ _____ (specialty) in the state of _____, the physician shall immediately take any and all action necessary to obtain such license. The physician shall maintain such license in the state of _____ in good standing throughout the term of this agreement.
   c. The physician shall immediately apply for active status on the medical staff of the hospital. The physician shall maintain such active status on the medical staff in good standing

throughout the term of this agreement and shall comply with all provisions of the medical staff bylaws of the hospital as well as any other rules or regulations issued by the hospital governing its medical staff.

d. The physician shall establish and maintain in accordance with generally accepted accounting principles an accounting and billing system with respect to his or her practice. He or she shall maintain such books and records as shall be adequate to permit the hospital to confirm the billings and collections related to the practice during all periods relevant to this agreement. The physician shall permit the hospital to inspect and make extracts from or copies of his/her books and records from time to time. The physician shall permit the hospital at least monthly to conduct an audit and reconciliation of the books and records of his or her practice for all periods relevant to this agreement and the physician agrees to cooperate fully in the conduct of such audits.

e. The physician shall maintain malpractice insurance with the minimum limits of 1 Million/3 Million dollars throughout the term of this agreement. Upon the request of the hospital from time to time the physician shall show adequate proof of such insurance.

f. At all times during the effectiveness of this agreement, the physician shall pursue his or her practice on a full-time basis and shall in good faith use his/her best efforts to develop a successful practice. The physician shall use his/her best efforts to collect billings from his/her practice.

2. *Obligations of the Hospital*

a. Contingent upon the physician's fulfillment of his/her obligations under this agreement and subject to the limitations herein set forth, the hospital hereby guarantees that the gross receipts (as hereinafter defined) from the physician's practice as established pursuant to section 1(a) hereof shall be no less than _____ (hereinafter referred to as the guaranteed amount) during the initial year (and hereinafter defined) of the physician's practice of _____ in the area of the hospital.

b. For the purpose of this agreement, the term "Gross Receipts" shall mean the value of monies, goods or services actually or constructively received by the physician as a result of his or her practice without reduction or offset for expenses, to include laboratory services, depreciation, taxes, or otherwise. In addition, the term "Gross Receipts" shall include all accounts receivable from the practice which are or should be reflected on the books and records of the practice on the last day of the initial year, but only to the extent that such amounts are collected within 90 days of such date.

c. For the purpose of this agreement the term "Initial Year" shall be a period of 365 (numerical 365) consecutive days commencing on the first day of the month immediately after all of the following requirements are met.

(1) The physician is duly licensed to practice_____ _____ in the state of _____ .

(2) The physician is an active member in good standing on the medical staff of the hospital.

(3) The physician has obtained an office suitably equipped and furnished from which to conduct his or her practice and has hired such employees as may be needed to assist in his or her practice.

(4) The physician has actually commenced his or her practice by holding himself or herself out as a practicing _____ .

3. Method of Payment

a. The hospital shall pay to the physician the amount by which the guaranteed amount exceeds the gross receipts for the initial year.

b. The total amount to be paid pursuant to section 3(A) hereof shall be paid in twelve (numerical 12) monthly installments which shall be subject to adjustment as set forth below. Each monthly installment shall be due on or before the last day of each calendar month during the initial year. The amount of the first payment shall be one-twelfth (1/12) of the guaranteed amount. The amount of each subsequent payment shall be reduced by the total gross receipts from the immediate month.

   c. No later than one-hundred twenty (120) days following the end of the initial year, the physician shall pay to the hospital the amount by which the total installments paid pursuant to section (B) exceed the amount to which the physician is entitled under section 3(A). If the excess is not paid when due, it shall bear interest at the highest rate permitted by law until paid. Payment of the total debt to the hospital must be made prior to the end of six (6) months.

4. Change in Terms

   a. The hospital may in its sole discretion, but only with the physician's consent, extend the initial year up to an additional twelve (12) months and the hospital may elect to modify the guaranteed amount for the extended period. In the event of such extension, the definitions of initial year and guaranteed amount shall be amended by execution of a written memorandum setting forth what the new extended initial year and modified amount shall be.

   b. In the event that the physician breeches this agreement (by ceasing to satisfy all of the criteria set forth in section 1 hereof, or otherwise) or for any reasons whatsoever terminates (whether temporarily or permanently) his or her practice, then the initial year shall immediately terminate without notice notwithstanding any provision of this agreement to the contrary. In addition, the guaranteed amount shall be prorated to reflect the shorter initial year. Such termination shall be an addition to and not in lieu of any other remedy the hospital may have. For the purpose of this section, a short-term illness or incapacity shall not be treated as termination of the physician's practice and a short-term illness or incapacity shall be one which does not or is not expected to keep the physician from his or her full-time practice for more than sixty (60) days.

5. Support Services

In addition to payment of the guaranteed amount, the hospital shall assist the physician in defraying the cost of establishing his or her practice as follows:

The hospital shall pay or reimburse the physician for the reasonable moving expenses of the physician as follows:

    a. The travel and lodging, (not to exceed five (5) days), expenses of the physician and his or her spouse from their current residence to the vicinity of the hospital for the purpose of becoming familiar with residential areas near the hospital and locating a new residence.

    b. The travel and lodging, (not to exceed five (5) days), expenses of the physician and his immediate family incurred from moving from their current residence to the new residence near the hospital.

    c. The normal and usual expenses of moving the physician's household furnishings and personal belongings from his or her current residence to his or her new residence near the hospital not to exceed _____ .

6. Remedies

In the event that the physician shall breech this agreement, he or she shall repay to the hospital all amounts expended by the hospital pursuant to this agreement, together with interest thereon from the date of payment to or for the benefit of the physician. Until paid, such interest is to be at the highest rate permitted by law. This remedy shall be in addition to and not in lieu of any other remedy available to the hospital.

7. Relationship

There is no relationship of employer-employee, independent contractor, principal-agent, or partnerships established by this agreement. Moreover, the physician's eligibility for medical staff privileges at the hospital is not governed by this agreement and this agreement does not in any way modify the medical staff bylaws or any governing provisions. The sole purpose of this agreement is to induce the physician to establish his or her practice in the area of the hospital because of the

hospital's belief that there is an insufficient practicing
_____ (specialty) in this area.

8. *Access to Book and Records*

Upon the written request of the Secretary of Health and Human Services or the Controller General or any of their duly authorized representatives, the physician will make available to those persons contracts, books, documents, and records necessary to verify the nature and extent of the cost of providing services under this agreement. Such inspection shall be available up to four (4) years after rendering such services. If the physician carries out any other duties of this agreement through a sub-contract with a value of $10,000 or more over a twelve-(12) month period with a related individual or organization, the physician agrees to include this requirement in any such subcontract. This section is included pursuant to, and is governed by, the requirement of public law 96-499 Section 952(section 1861 internal) the (one of the Social Security Act) and the regulations promulgated thereunder. No attorney-client accountant-client or other legal privilege will redeem to have been waived by the hospital or the physician by virtue of this agreement.

9. *Non-Discrimination*

The physician shall not discriminate on the basis of race, color, sex, age, religion, national origin or handicap in providing services under this agreement or in the section of associate employees or independent contractors.

10. *Regulatory Requirement*

The hospital and the physician shall operate at all times in compliance with federal, state and local laws, rules and regulations, the policies, rules and regulations of the hospital, the applicable standards of the joint commission on the accreditation of healthcare organizations and all currently accepted approved methods and practices of medicine.

11. *Hold Harmless*

a. The physician will indemnify and hold the hospital harmless from any and all claims, actions, liability and expenses (including costs of judgments, settlements, court costs and attorneys fees regardless of the outcome of such claim or action) caused by, resulting from, or alleging negligent, or intentional acts or omissions or any failure to perform any obligations undertaken, or any covenant in this agreement whether such act, omission or failure was the physician's or that of any person providing services hereunder, through or for the physician. Upon notice from the hospital, the physician shall resist and defend, at his own expense, and by counsel reasonably satisfactory to the hospital, any such claim or action. The physician shall carry proper insurance with the hospital as an additional named insured to the extent that such insurance is reasonably available.

b. The hospital will indemnify and hold the physician harmless from any and all claims, actions, liability or expenses (including costs of settlements, judgments, court costs and attorneys fees regardless of the outcome of such claim or action) caused by, resulting from, or alleging the negligent, or intentional actions or omissions of the hospital employees, or any failure to perform any obligation undertaken, or any covenant made by the hospital under this agreement. Upon notice from the physician, the hospital will resist and defend, at its own expense, and by counsel reasonably satisfactory to the physician any such claim or action.

12. *Notices*

Any notices permitted or required by this agreement shall be deemed made on the day personally delivered in writing or deposited in the US Mail's postage pre-paid to the other party at the address set forth below or to another address designated by the party by notice consistent with this section:

If to the physician _____

_____

_____

If to the hospital ——————————————————————

————————————————————————————————————

————————————————————————————————————

The interpretation and enforcement of this agreement shall be governed by the internal laws (without reference to conflict of laws, provisions) of the state of _____ .

13. Serviceability
The invalidity or unenforceability of any provision of this agreement shall not affect the validity or enforceability of any other provision.

14. Assignability
The right and obligation of the hospital hereunder shall inure to the benefit of and be binding upon the successors and assigns of the hospital. The physician may not assign his/her rights or obligations under this agreement except that the physician shall be required to assign this agreement to any corporate entity succeeding to the practice and shall promptly give the hospital notice of such assignment.

15. Amendments
Any amendments to this agreement will be effective only if in writing and signed by the hospital and the physician.

16. Entire Agreement
This agreement constitutes the entire agreement of the parties with respect to the subject matter thereof.

17. Interpretation
The defined terms used herein are for convenience only and do not limit the contents of this agreement.

18. Name Change
This agreement shall continue in full force and effect should a change in the name of the hospital occur.

19. No Waiver

No waiver of a breech of any provision of this agreement shall be construed to be a waiver of any breech of any other provision. No delay in acting with regard to any breech of any provision of this agreement shall be construed to be a waiver of such breech.

20. Variations of Pronouns

All pronouns and all variations thereof shall be deemed to refer to the masculine, feminine or neuter, singular or plural as the identity of the person or persons or entity may require.

21. Authorization for Agreement

The execution and performance of this agreement by physician and hospital have been duly authorized by all necessary laws, resolutions or corporate action and this agreement constitutes the valid and enforceable obligation of physician and hospital in accordance with its terms.

In witness whereof hospital has caused its name to be hereunto subscribed by a duly authorized officer thereunto and physician had hereunto subscribed his/her name as of the day and year first above written _____ , MD.

By:

_____

Hospital Administrator

PHYSICIAN RECRUITMENT AGREEMENT: EXAMPLE 2

This agreement is made and entered into this ____ day of _____ 199__ by and between _____ a non-profit corporation (hereinafter "hospital") and _____ , M.D. (hereinafter "physician") *witness whereas* hospital operates a hospital at _____ (cities), _____ (state), known as _____ hospital; and *whereas* it is in the best interest of the hospital and in furtherance of its primary purpose of providing patient care to the sick that physicians be available in the _____ (city) area and in particular the _____ (county) *whereas* physician is willing to relocate to the _____ (county) in _____ (state) on the terms and conditions hereinafter set forth; *now therefore* in consideration of the premised, it is agreed:

1. Physician represents that he or she is a _____ physician duly licensed to practice as such in the state of _____.

2. Physician agrees to move to _____ (county) establishing his/her residence within _____ (county) and to establish and maintain for a period of one year or until he or she repays hospital all funds to be reimbursed by him or her pursuant to this agreement whichever is longer. His or her main office for the practice of his or her profession as a _____ physician which said office shall be in the _____ area of _____ (county). The period of one year shall commence the date the physician opens his or her main office in the _____ area of _____ (county) _____ (state) for the practice of his or her profession.

3. Physician agrees to apply for admission to the medical staff of _____ hospital by _____, 199___ or such extensions as may be agreed to by the parties. Physician shall maintain his membership on the medical staff of _____ hospital for a period of five (5) years from and after the date of his or her first admission. Physician shall comply with the bylaws of such medical staff and serve on committees in accordance to their width.

4. It is understood and agreed that the hospital is not permitted to practice medicine and that in order to properly achieve its

purpose of providing care for the sick in the _____,
(county) it is in the best interest of the hospital to have a
physician establish his or her office in the _____
_____ area of _____ (county) and serve on
committees thereof.

5. Hospital agrees to pay up to _____ dollars for physician's
   expenses in moving his or her household furniture and furnish-
   ings from his or her present residence in _____
   (city). _____ (state) to _____ (county)
   and his or her expenses in moving any necessary office fur-
   nishings from physicians present office to _____
   (county) _____ (state) including verified personal expenses for physician incurred in connection with the move for
   lodging and meals. Hospital will pay the moving expenses
   directly to _____ which will be employed to move
   the personal property herein referred to. Hospital shall reimburse physician directly for such verified lodging and meals,
   provided, however, the total amount paid to physician under
   this paragraph shall not exceed $ _____. The cost and
   expenses referred to in this paragraph need not be reimbursed
   by physician to hospital.

6. Hospital shall reimburse physician for his or her office rental
   not exceeding $_____ per month for the first twelve (12)
   months after office rental begins in the _____
   area of _____ (county) (state) _____.

7. Hospital shall purchase the medical equipment as described on
   exhibit A hereto such equipment to be located in and used at
   physician's medical office in the _____ area of
   _____ (county) (state) _____. Physician shall
   reimburse hospital for the purchase of such equipment by
   paying to hospital one-half of the amounts charged to patients
   for use of such equipment.

8. Hospital will underwrite by guarantee or other instrument required by _____ bank for the benefit of physician to the extent of $_____ in interest upon which shall

be at the rate of _____ per cent per annum. This line of credit established for a period beginning upon the execution of this contract and continuing until one (1) year after opening the physician's _____ area office. During said period, hospital shall pay the interest due to _____ _____ bank. The interest paid by the hospital up to the limit of _____ percent per annum shall be reimbursed by physician to hospital by being added to the amount of credit extended to physician. Physician shall execute and deliver a note to _____ bank in the amount of the drawings of physician against the line of credit. The note shall be in the form in use by _____ bank and shall bear interest at _____ percent per annum with payments thereon to be made in six (6) monthly installments commencing at the end of one (1) year after physician opens his or her office in the _____ area of _____ (county), _____ (state). If as a result of physician's default, hospital is required to pay any amounts due under said note to _____ bank, then physician shall reimburse hospital for same. Hospital shall execute such documents as may be required by _____ bank to guarantee said line of credit.

9. Hospital shall further pay to the physician, the sum of $_____ per month for a twelve-(12) month period commencing _____, 199__. This payment shall be a minimum guarantee to physician for such one-(1) year period and shall be reimbursed by physician to hospital to the following extent and in the following manner.
   a. Within fifteen (15) days after the end of each quarter of said one-(1) year period, the amount of physician's net income for the quarter as defined in subparagraph (b) shall be paid by physician to hospital. In the event receipts and expenses attributable to services rendered during any quarter cannot be determined within the said fifteen-(15) day period upon estimate with adjustments to be made upon final determination.

b. Net income under subparagraph 9(a) shall be determined as follows. All receipts by physicians for services rendered during the period (excluding the $_____ per month payment from the hospital) less all expenses of operation of physician's offices in the _____ area, actually paid for said period (excluding expense paid by hospital hereunder and not reimbursed by physician).

c. Amounts reimbursed by physician shall not exceed the total of $_____.

Notwithstanding the foregoing, hospitals shall make no payments to physician under this paragraph for any periods during which physician is disabled and payments are made under the disability policy described in paragraph 10(b) below.

10. To secure repayment to hospital of obligations payable by physician hereunder and to reimburse hospital for amounts paid hereunder in the event of death or disability of physician, hospital shall procure and pay for policies of insurance from insurance companies of hospital's choice as follows:

a. A term policy of life insurance insuring the life of a physician in the sum of $_____ which said policy shall be assigned to hospital. No part of the proceeds of this policy need be paid or accounted for by hospital to physician or his or her heirs, devisees or legatees.

b. A disability insurance policy insuring physician, providing for payment because of physician's disability in the sum of $_____ per month during any period he or she is unable by reason of illness or disability to practice as a _____ _____ physician in _____ (county) _____ (state). Fifty percent (50%) of the proceeds paid by such policy shall be paid directly to physician. No part of the hospital's portion of the proceeds of this policy need be repaid by hospital to physician. All proceeds received by hospital under this disability or illness policy shall be retained by hospital for its own use and benefit.

11. If physician fails to maintain his or her main office for the practice of medicine as _____ physician in the _____ area of _____

(county) for the period of one (1) year or until he/she repays the hospital and or _____ bank all sums payable by physician hereunder in full, whichever last occurs, then notwithstanding the provisions of any promissory note, hospital and or _____ bank shall have the right to declare all amounts due from physician under para- graph 8 to be immediately due and payable.

12. In the event physician fails within one (1) year from the time he or she opens his or her professional offices in the area _____ of _____ (county) as provided herein to maintain his or her principal office for the practice of medicine in said office, he or she shall assign the lease of the office premises, together with any lease on the equipment referred to herein, to hospital which shall thereafter pay and perform the terms and obligations of said leases.

13. The relationship between the parties hereto is that of indepen- dent contractor. Neither party shall have any right to direct or control the activities of the other whether in the performance of this agreement or otherwise. Sums payable hereunder to physician are not as compensation for services.

14. Physician agrees to allow hospital access to his or her books of account and other records to enable hospital to verify physi- cian's net income. Such access shall be allowed to hospital during regular business hours.

15. Physician understands and agrees to the access provisions of section 952 of the Omnibus Reconciliation Act of 1980 (Pub- lic Law 96-499) and the implementing regulations.

16. This agreement may be terminated by hospital upon the hap- pening of any of the following:
   a. death of the physician.
   b. physician becomes permanently disabled as a result of which he or she is unable to practice medicine.
   c. physician's license to practice medicine is suspended or re- voked, or

    d. physician fails to apply for or attain or maintain member-
ship in the _____ hospital medical staff.

17. Physician may terminate this agreement if _____
_____ hospital:
a. fails to obtain renewal of accreditation by JCAHO, or
b. fails to continue to be licensed as an acute care hospital.

18. In the event of termination of this agreement under paragraph
16, hospital/_____ bank shall have the right
to declare all sums due to it or them hereunder from physician
immediately due and payable, notwithstanding the due date set
forth on any promissory note representing such obligations. In
the event of termination of this agreement under paragraph 17,
physician's obligation shall remain as set forth under paragraph
8 and shall not be accelerated by reason of such termination.

19. In any event this agreement shall expire six (6) years after the
date the physician first opens his or her office for the practice
of medicine as a _____ physician in _____
_____ (county) provided however that all obligations to be reimbursed to hospital by physician as provided
herein shall survive the termination of this agreement, whether
such termination is pursuant to the paragraph, paragraph
16/paragraph 17. *In witness whereof,* this agreement is
executed by the parties hereto the day and year first above
written.

_____ Hospital

By its _____

"Hospital"

_____

MD "Physician"

VERIFICATION OF NOTARY PUBLIC OF THE SIGNING OF PHYSICIAN RECRUITMENT AGREEMENTS

State of _____

County of _____

I _____, Notary Public, do hereby

certify that _____ MD personally ap-
peared before me this day and executed the foregoing instrument.

This the _____ day of _____ , 199___.

_____ Notary Public

My commission expires _____.

State of _____

County of _____

I _____, Notary Public, do hereby certify that

_____, administrator of _____

hospital personally appeared before me this day and executed the
foregoing instrument.

This the _____ day of _____ , 199___.

_____ Notary Public

My commission expires _____.

Appendix A: Medical Schools

Alabama

University of Alabama-Birmingham
School of Medicine
University Station
Birmingham, AL 35294
James Pittman Jr., MD, Dean
(205) 934-5391

University of South Alabama
School of Medicine
Medical Sciences Building
Mobile, AL 36688
Charles M. Baugh, MD, Dean
(205) 460-7187

Arizona

University of Arizona
College of Medicine
Arizona Health Sciences Center
Tucson, AZ 85724
James E. Dalen, MD, Dean
(602) 626-7383

Arkansas

University of Arkansas
College of Medicine
4301 West Markham Street
Little Rock, AR 72205
Dodd Wilson, MD, Dean
(501) 686-5350

California

**Charles R. Drew University
of Medicine & Science**
1621 East 120th Street
Los Angeles, CA 90059
Lewis King, MD, Dean
(213) 563-4974

**Loma Linda University
School of Medicine**
Loma Linda, CA 92350
A. Douglas Will, MD, Dean
(714) 824-4462

**Stanford University
School of Medicine**
851 Welch Road
Palo Alto, CA 94304
David Korn, MD, Dean
(415) 723-6436

**University of California-Davis
School of Medicine**
Davis, CA 95616
Hibbard Williams, MD, Dean
(916) 752-0321

**University of California-Irvine
California College of Medicine**
Irvine, CA 92717
Walter L. Henry, MD, Dean
(714) 856-6119

**University of California-Los Angeles
UCLA School of Medicine**
Los Angeles, CA 90024
Kenneth I. Shine, MD, Dean
(213) 825-5851

University of California-San Diego
School of Medicine
La Jolla, CA 92093
Gerard N. Burrow, MD, Dean
(619) 534-1501

University of California-San Francisco
School of Medicine
San Francisco, CA 94143
Joseph B. Martin, MD, PhD, Dean
(415) 476-2342

University of Southern California
School of Medicine
2025 Zonal Avenue
Los Angeles, CA 90033
Stephen J. Ryan, MD, Dean
(213) 342-1544

Colorado

University of Colorado
School of Medicine
4200 East Ninth Avenue
Denver, CO 80262
Richard Krugman, MD, Dean
(303) 270-7563

Connecticut

University of Connecticut
School of Medicine
Farmington Avenue
Farmington, CT 06032
Eugene Sigma, MD, Dean
(203) 679-2413

Yale University
School of Medicine
333 Cedar Street
New Haven, CT 06510
Robert M. Donaldson Jr., MD, Acting Dean
(203) 785-4672

District of Columbia

George Washington University
School of Medicine & Health Sciences
2300 I Street, N.W.
Washington, DC 20037
Robert I. Keimowitz, MD, Dean
(202) 994-2987

Georgetown University
School of Medicine
3900 Reservoir Road, N.W.
Washington, DC 20007
William C. Maxted, MD, Academic Dean
(202) 687-1612

Howard University
College of Medicine
520 W. Street, N.W.
Washington, DC 20059
Charles H. Epps Jr., MD, Dean
(202) 806-6270

Florida

Florida State University
Program in Medical Sciences
Tallahassee, FL 32306
Robert Reeves, PhD, Director
(904) 644-1855

University of Florida
College of Medicine
J. Hillis Miller Health Center
Gainesville, FL 32610
Allen H. Neims, MD, PhD, Dean
(904) 392-5397

University of Miami
School of Medicine
P.O. Box 016159
Miami, FL 33101
Bernard J. Fogel, MD, Dean
(305) 547-6545

University of South Florida
College of Medicine
12901 North 30th Street
Tampa, FL 33612
Marvin R. Dunn, MD, Dean
(813) 974-4950

Georgia

Emory University
School of Medicine
Woodruff Medical Center
Administration Building
Atlanta, GA 30322
Jeffrey Houpt, MD, Dean
(404) 727-5630

Medical College of Georgia
School of Medicine
Augusta, GA 30912
Gregory L. Eastwood, MD, Dean
(404) 721-2231

Mercer University
School of Medicine
Macon, GA 31207
Douglas Skelton, MD, Dean
(912) 752-2532

Morehouse School of Medicine
720 Westview Drive, S.W.
Atlanta, GA 30310
Dewitt Alfred, MD, Dean
(404) 752-1728

Hawaii

University of Hawaii
John A. Burns School of Medicine
1960 East-West Road
Honolulu, HI 96822
Christian L. Gulbrandsen, MD, Dean
(808) 956-8287

Illinois

Loyola University of Chicago
Stritch School of Medicine
2160 South 1st Avenue
Maywood, IL 60153
Daniel H. Winship, MD, Dean
(708) 216-3223

Northwestern University Medical School
303 East Chicago Avenue
Chicago, IL 60611
Harry Beaty, MD, Dean
(312) 503-8186

Rush Medical College of Rush University
600 South Paulina Street
Chicago, IL 60612
Roger C. Bone, MD, Acting Dean
(312) 942-5269

Southern Illinois University
School of Medicine
801 North Rutledge Street
Springfield, IL 62702
Richard Moy, MD, Dean
(217) 782-3318

University of Chicago
Pritzker School of Medicine
5724 South Ellis Avenue
Chicago, IL 60637
Samuel Hellman, MD, Dean
(312) 702-9000

University of Health Sciences
Chicago Medical School
3333 Green Bay Road
North Chicago, IL 60064
Theodore Booden, PhD, Acting Dean
(708) 578-3300

University of Illinois
College of Medicine
1853 West Polk Street
Chicago, IL 60612
Gerald Moss, MD, Dean
(312) 996-3500

University of Illinois
College of Medicine
Peoria School of Medicine
1 Illini Drive
Peoria, IL 61656
Michael Bailie, MD, Director
(309) 671-8402

Kentucky

University of Kentucky
College of Medicine
800 Rose Street
Lexington, KY 40536
Emery A. Wilson, MD, Dean
(606) 233-6582

University of Louisville
School of Medicine
Health Sciences Center
Louisville, KY 40292
Donald Kmetz, MD, Dean
(502) 588-5184

Louisiana

Louisiana State University
School of Medicine in New Orleans
1542 Tulane Avenue
New Orleans, LA 70112
Robert Daniels, MD, Dean
(504) 568-4006

Louisiana State University
School of Medicine in Shreveport
P.O. Box 33932
Shreveport, LA 71130
Ike Muslow, MD, Acting Dean
(318) 674-5240

Tulane University
School of Medicine
1430 Tulane Avenue
New Orleans, LA 70112
Vincent A. Fulginiti, MD, Dean
(504) 588-5462

Maryland

Johns Hopkins University
School of Medicine
720 Rutland Avenue
Baltimore, MD 21205
Michael E. Johns, MD, Dean
(301) 955-3180

**Uniformed Services University
of the Health Sciences
School of Medicine**
4301 Jones Bridge Road
Bethesda, MD 20814
Harry C. Holloway, MD, Acting Dean
(301) 295-3016

**University of Maryland
School of Medicine**
655 West Baltimore Street
Baltimore, MD 21201
Donald E. Wilson, MD, Dean
(410) 328-7410

Massachusetts

**Boston University
School of Medicine**
80 East Concord Street
Boston, MA 02118
Aram Chobanian, MD, Dean
(617) 638-5300

Harvard Medical School
25 Shattuck Street
Boston, MA 02115
Daniel Tosteson, MD, Dean
(617) 432-1501

**Tufts University
School of Medicine**
136 Harrison Avenue
Boston, MA 02111
Richard M. Ryan, MD, Acting Dean
(617) 956-6565

University of Massachusetts Medical School
55 Lake Avenue, North
Worcester, MA 01605
Aaron Lazare, MD, Dean
(508) 856-0011

Michigan

Michigan State University
College of Human Medicine
East Lansing, MI 48824
William Abbett, PhD, Dean
(517) 353-1730

University of Michigan Medical School
1301 Catherine Road
Ann Arbor, MI 48109
Giles G. Bole, MD, Dean
(313) 763-1468

Wayne State University
School of Medicine
540 East Canfield Avenue
Detroit, MI 48201
Robert Sokol, MD, Dean
(313) 577-1335

Minnesota

Mayo Medical School
200 First Street, S.W.
Rochester, MN 55905
Burton Sandok, MD, Dean
(507) 284-8635

University of Minnesota-Duluth
School of Medicine
2400 Oakland Avenue
Duluth, MN 55812
Ron Franks, MD, Dean
(218) 726-7572

University of Minnesota
Medical School-Minneapolis
Minneapolis, MN 55455
David M. Brown, MD, Dean
(612) 626-4949

Mississippi

**University of Mississippi
School of Medicine**
2500 North State Street
Jackson, MS 39216
Norma Nelson, MD, Dean
(601) 984-1010

Missouri

**Saint Louis University
School of Medicine**
1402 South Grand Boulevard
St. Louis, MO 63104
William Stoneman III, MD, Dean
(314) 577-8201

**University of Missouri-Columbia
School of Medicine**
Hospital Drive
Columbia, MO 65212
Lester R. Bryant, MD, Dean
(314) 882-1566

**University of Missouri-Kansas City
School of Medicine**
5100 Rockhill Road
Kansas City, MO 64110
James Mongan, MD, Dean
(816) 235-1808

**Washington University
School of Medicine**
660 South Euclid Avenue
St. Louis, MO 63110
William A. Peck, MD, Dean
(314) 362-6827

Nebraska

Creighton University
School of Medicine
California at 24th Street
Omaha, NE 68178
Richard O'Brien, MD, Dean
(402) 280-2600

University of Nebraska
College of Medicine
42nd Street and Dewey Avenue
Omaha, NE 68105
Layton Rikkers, MD, Interim Dean
(402) 559-4204

Nevada

University of Nevada
School of Medicine
Reno, NV 89557
Robert Daugherty Jr., MD, PhD, Dean
(702) 784-6001

New Hampshire

Dartmouth Medical School
Hanover, NH 03756
Andrew G. Wallace, MD, Dean
(603) 646-7480

New Jersey

UMD-Rutgers Medical School at Camden
300 Broadway Street
Camden, NJ 08103
Gordon D. Benson, MD, Dean
(609) 757-7877

University of Medicine & Dentistry of NJ
New Jersey Medical School
100 Bergen Street
Newark, NJ 07103
Ruy V. Lourenzo, MD, Dean
(201) 456-4539

University of Medicine & Dentistry of NJ
Rutgers Medical School
P.O. Box 101
Piscataway, NJ 08854
Norma H. Edelman, MD, Dean
(908) 463-4557

New Mexico

University of New Mexico
School of Medicine
Albuqucrquo, NM 87131
Leonard Napolitano, MD, Dean
(505) 277-2321

New York

Albert Einstein College of Medicine
of Yeshiva University
1300 Morris Park Avenue
New York, NY 10461
Dominick Purpura, MD, Dean
(212) 430-2801

Albany Medical College of Union University
47 New Scotland Avenue
Albany, NY 12208
Anthony Tartaglia, MD, Dean
(518) 445-5544

Columbia University
College of Physicians and Surgeons
630 West 168th Street
New York, NY 10032
Herbert Pardes, MD, Dean
(212) 305-3595

Cornell University
Medical College
445 East 69th Street
New York, NY 10021
Robert Michels, MD, Dean
(212) 746-6005

Mount Sinai School of Medicine
of the City University of New York
1 Gustave L. Levy Place
New York, NY 10029
Nathan Case, MD, Dean
(212) 241-6696

New York Medical College
Elmwood Hall
Valhalla, NY 10595
Karl P. Adler, MD, Dean
(914) 993-4500

New York University
School of Medicine
550 First Avenue
New York, NY 10016
Saul Farber, MD, Dean
(212) 263-5372

University of Rochester
School of Medicine and Dentistry
601 Elmwood Avenue
Rochester, NY 14642
Marshall Lichtman, MD, Dean
(716) 275-0017

State University of New York at Buffalo
School of Medicine
Buffalo, NY 14214
John Naughton, MD, Dean
(716) 831-2775

State University of New York
Health Science Center at Brooklyn
College of Medicine
450 Clarkson Avenue
Brooklyn, NY 11203
Irwin M. Weiner, MD, Dean
(718) 270-3776

State University of New York at Stony Brook
Health Sciences Center
School of Medicine
Stony Brook, NY 11794
Jordan J. Cohen, MD, Dean
(516) 444-2080

State University of New York
Health Science Center at Syracuse
College of Medicine
750 E. Adam Street
Syracuse, NY 13210
William J. Williams, MD, Dean
(315) 464-4515

North Carolina

Bowman Gray School of Medicine
of Wake Forest University
Medical Center Boulevard
Winston-Salem, NC 27157-1003
Richard Janeway, MD, Dean
(919) 748-4424

Duke University
School of Medicine
P.O. Box 3710
Durham, NC 27710
Doyle G. Graham, MD, PhD, Dean
(919) 684-2498

East Carolina University
School of Medicine
Greenville, SC 27834
James A. Hallock, MD, Dean
(919) 551-2201

University of North Carolina at Chapel Hill
School of Medicine
Chapel Hill, NC 27514
Stuart Bondurant, MD, Dean
(919) 966-4161

North Dakota

University of North Dakota
School of Medicine
501 Columbia Road
Grand Forks, ND 58201
Edwin C. James, MD, Dean
(701) 777-2514

Ohio

Case Western Reserve University
School of Medicine
2119 Abington Road
Cleveland, OH 44106
Neil Cherniack, MD, Dean
(216) 368-2820

Medical College of Ohio at Toledo
Caller Service No. 10008
Toledo, OH 43699
Richard F. Leighton, MD, Dean
(419) 381-4242

Northeastern Ohio Universities
College of Medicine
Rootstown, OH 44272
Colin Campbell, MD, Dean
(216) 325-2511

Ohio State University
College of Medicine
370 West Ninth Avenue
Columbus, OH 43210
Manuel Tzagournis, MD, Dean
(614) 292-0926

Wright State University
P.O. Box 1751
Dayton, OH 45401
Kim Goldenberg, MD, Dean
(513) 873-2933

University of Cincinnati
College of Medicine
231 Bethesda Avenue
Cincinnati, OH 45267
John J. Hutton Jr., MD, Dean
(513) 558-7391

Oklahoma

University of Oklahoma
College of Medicine
P.O. Box 26901
Oklahoma City, OK 73190
Edward N. Brandt Jr., MD, PhD, Dean
(405) 271-2265

University of Oklahoma-Tulsa
Medical College
2808 South Sheridan Street
Tulsa, OK 74129
Daniel C. Plunket, MD, Interim Dean
(918) 838-4695

Oregon

Oregon Health Sciences University
School of Medicine
3181 S.W. Sam Jackson Park Road
Portland, OR 97201
John A. Benson, MD, Interim Dean
(503) 494-8220

Pennsylvania

Hannemann University
School of Medicine
245 North 15th Street
Philadelphia, PA 19102
Steven Risen, MD, Interim Dean
(215) 448-7604

Jefferson Medical College
of Thomas Jefferson University
1025 Walnut Street
Philadelphia, PA 19107
Joseph S. Gonnella, MD, Dean
(215) 955-6980

Medical College of Pennsylvania
3300 Henry Avenue
Philadelphia, PA 19129
Leonard Ross, PhD, Dean
(215) 842-7007

Milton S. Hershey Medical Center
Pennsylvania State University
College of Medicine
P.O. Box 850
Hershey, PA 17033
C. McCollister Evarts, MD, Dean
(717) 531-8323

Temple University
School of Medicine
Broad and Ontario Streets
Philadelphia, PA 19140
Allen R. Myers, MD, Dean
(215) 221-4019

University of Pennsylvania
School of Medicine
Philadelphia, PA 19104
William N. Kelley, MD, Dean
(215) 898-5181

University of Pittsburgh
School of Medicine
Pittsburgh, PA 15261
George M. Bernier Jr., MD, Dean
(412) 648-8975

Rhode Island

Brown University
Program in Medicine
Providence, RI 02912
David S. Greer, MD, Dean
(401) 863-3330

South Carolina

Medical University of South Carolina
College of Medicine
171 Ashley Avenue
Charleston, SC 29425
Layton McCurdy, MD, Dean
(803) 792-2081

University of South Carolina
School of Medicine
Columbia, SC 29208
J. O'Neal Humphries, MD, Dean
(803) 733-3200

South Dakota

> **University of South Dakota**
> **School of Medicine**
> Vermillion, SD 57069
> Robert C. Talley, MD, Dean
> (605) 339-6648

Tennessee

> **East Tennessee State University**
> **Quillen-Dishner College of Medicine**
> P.O. Box 19900A
> Johnson City, TN 37614
> Paul Stanton Jr., MD, Dean
> (615) 929-6315

> **Meharry Medical College**
> **School of Medicine**
> 1005 D.B. Todd Jr. Boulevard
> Nashville, TN 37208
> Henry W. Foster, MD, Dean
> (615) 327-6204

> **University of Tennessee**
> **Center for the Health Sciences**
> **College of Medicine**
> 800 Madison Avenue
> Memphis, TN 38163
> Robert Summit, MD, Dean
> (901) 528-5529

> **Vanderbilt University**
> **School of Medicine**
> Nashville, TN 37232
> John Chapman, MD, Dean
> (615) 322-2164

Texas

Baylor University
Texas Medical Center
Houston, TX 77030
John C. Riddle, MD, Dean
(713) 792-5000

Texas A & M University
College of Medicine
College Station, TX 77843
Richard A. DeVaul, MD, Dean
(409) 845-3431

Texas Tech University
Health Sciences Center
School of Medicine
4th Street and Indiana Avenue
Lubbock, TX 79430
Darryl Williams, MD, Dean
(806) 743-3000

University of Texas
Medical School at Galveston
Galveston, TX 77550
George Bryan, MD, Dean
(409) 772-2671

University of Texas
Medical School at Houston
P.O. Box 20708
Houston, TX 77025
John C. Ribble, MD, Dean
(713) 792-5000

University of Texas
Medical School of San Antonio
7703 Floyd Curl Drive
San Antonio, TX 78284
James Young, PhD, Dean
(512) 567-4420

University of Texas
Southwestern Medical School at Dallas
5323 Harry Hines Boulevard
Dallas, TX 77550
William B. Neaves, PhD, Dean
(214) 688-2022

Utah

University of Utah
School of Medicine
50 North Medical Drive
Salt Lake City, UT 84132
Frank H. Tyler, MD, Acting Dean
(801) 581-6436

Vermont

University of Vermont
College of Medicine
Burlington, VT 05405
John W. Frymoyer, MD, Interim Dean
(802) 656-2156

Virginia

Eastern Virginia Medical School
700 Olney Road
Norfolk, VA 23501
James E. Etheridge Jr., MD, Dean
(804) 446-5800

University of Virginia
School of Medicine
Charlottesville, VA 22908
Robert M. Carey, MD, Dean
(804) 924-5118

Virginia Commonwealth University
Medical College of Virginia
School of Medicine
P.O. Box 565
MCV Station
Richmond, VA 23298
Stephen M. Ayres, MD, Dean
(804) 786-9788

Washington

University of Washington
School of Medicine
Seattle, WA 98195
Philip J. Fialkow, MD, Dean
(206) 543-1515

West Virginia

Marshall University
School of Medicine
1542 Spring Valley Drive
Huntington, WV 25704
Charles H. McKown, MD, Dean
(304) 696-7000

West Virginia University
School of Medicine
Morgantown, WV 26506
Robert M. D'Alessandri, MD, Dean
(304) 293-4511

Wisconsin

Medical College of Wisconsin
8701 West Watertown Plank Road
Milwaukee, WI 53226
Richard A. Cooper, MD, Dean
(414) 257-8213

University of Wisconsin
Medical School
1300 University Avenue
Madison, WI 53706
Laurence J. Marton, MD, Dean
(608) 263-4910

Appendix B:
Other Sources

Residency Programs

For a directory listing of residency programs and fellowships for all specialties in the United States, and its possessions, call the Accreditation Council for Graduate Medical Education (ACGME) at (312) 464-4920.

For information on physicians in residency programs by specialty, contact the following people:

- Judith Armbruster, PhD (312-464-4642), or Thomas Kulik (312-464- 4645) for:

  Anesthesiology
  Nuclear Medicine
  Radiology

- John T. Boberg, PhD (312-464-4687), or Marsha Stojek (312-464- 4528) for:

  Ophthalmology
  Surgery
  Thoracic Surgery

- Glenna Case, PhD (312-464-5404), or Linda McClung (312-464- 5366) for:

  Emergency Medicine
  Neurological Surgery
  Plastic Surgery
  Psychiatry

- Paul O'Connor, PhD (312-464-4683), or Sheila Hart (312-464-4679) for:

  Colon and Rectal Surgery
  Neurology
  Obstetrics-Gynecology
  Physical Medicine & Rehabilitation

- Mary Alice Parsons (312-464-4947) or Steven McEllin (312-464-4945) for:

    Family Practice
    Pediatrics

- Steven Nestler, PhD (312-464-4692) or Marilyn Fitschen (312-464-4688) for:

    Dermatology
    Orthopedic Surgery
    Pathology

- Doris A. Stoll, PhD (312-464-5505) or Erma Long (312-464-5585) for:

    Allergy & Immunology
    Otolaryngology
    Preventive Medicine
    Urology

- Rachel Kohrman (312-464-4646) for:

    Internal Medicine

- Cynthia Taradejna (312-464-4685) or Constance Hyland (312-464-4684) for:

    Transitional Year Programs

- Philip Kenny, PhD (312-464-4948), Director for Field Staff Activities

- Rochella Ratliff, (312-464-4937), Coordinator for Specialist Site Visits

- Valeda Carbonneau (312-464-4942), Coordinator for Field Staff

- Penny Glover (312-464-4951), ACGME Administrative Secretary

- Barbara Warren (312-464-4939), ACGME Office Manager

- John Glenapp, PhD (312-464-4920), Executive Secretary, Accreditation Council for Graduate Medical Education

- Gary Grenholm, PhD (312-464-5331), Director, Data Systems– FREIDA

- James Weinlader, PhD (312-464-5405), Director for Residency Review Committee Activities

- Arthur Osteen, PhD (312-464-4677), Secretary of the Graduate Medical Education Advisory Committee (GMEAC)

- Hannah L. Hedrick, PhD (312-464-4697), Director of the Department of Information Analysis and Publications

- Sylvia I. Etzel (312-464-4693), Editor of the Directory of Graduate Medical Education Programs

Field staff representatives are:

- Bryant Galusha, MD, William Staples, MD, and Gertrude Stern, MD: Pediatrics
- Joseph Campisano, PhD: Education
- Irwin Cohen, MD: Internal Medicine
- Marianne Gideon, PhD: Health Education
- Francis Heck, MD and Newton Turk, III, MD: Thoracic Surgery
- David D. Smith, MD: Family Medicine
- Richard Johnson, EdD: Administration/Instruction
- George Lewis, MD: Preventive Medicine
- Christopher Pack, PhD: Sociology

National Organizations

For a directory listing of national organizations concerned with matters of interest to the healthcare field, send for the "American Hospital Association Guide to the Health Care Field." Cost is $70.00 for AHA institutional members ad $195.00 for nonmembers. Ask for product No. 010091. To order by telephone, call 1-800-242-2626; Visa, MasterCard, AMEX accepted. To order with a company purchase order, check or money order, mail to AHA Services, Inc., P.O. Box 92683, Chicago, IL 60675-2683.

Military Units

For a directory listing of military hospitals, contact the Uniformed Services for information on all their medical and dental facilities in the

United States and overseas. Send your request to: The Uniformed Services, Medical/Dental Facilities, American Forces Information Service, 1735 North Lynn Street, Room 210, Arlington, VA 22209-2086.

Federal Recruitment Sources

The following are federal recruitment sources:

Air Force Military Personnel Center
Randolph Air Force Base
Universal City, TX 78148

Commanding Officer
National Navy Medical Center
Bethesda, MD 20014

Director of Medical Education
Brook Army Medical Center
Fort Sam Houston
San Antonio, TX 78234

U.S. Public Health Service
5600 Fishers Lane
Rockville, MD 20857

Locum Tenens Organizations

The following is a listing of locum tenens organizations for temporary placement of physicians:

Comp Health
4021 South 700 East, Suite 300
Salt Lake City, UT 84107
(801) 264-6400

I.P.R.
7207 West Greenfield Street
Milwaukee, WI 53214
(414) 257-3959, within WI, or (800) 966-3627 within the U.S.

Locum Medical Group
3690 Orange Place, Suite 260
Beachwood, OH 44122
(216) 464-2125 or (800) 752-5515 within the U.S.

Kron Medical Locum Tenens
1400 Perimeter Park Drive
Morrisville, NC 27560
(800) 633-4225

MedStaff
2828 Croasdaile Drive
Durham, North Carolina 27705
(800) 476-4587, within NC, (919) 383-4075

Physician International Locum Tenens
4 Vermont Street
Buffalo, NY 14213-2498
(800) 622-4062

Interim Physician Network
1000 North Walnut Avenue, Suite B
New Braunfels, TX 78130
(800) 531-1122 or (512) 629-5858

Western States Physician Services
5627 E. Kings Canyon Road, Suite 156
Fresno, CA 93727
(209) 252-3047

AMA Placement Service

For a listing of physicians who are searching for positions, contact the American Medical Association Physician's Career Resource to register to receive a directory of physician candidate profiles. You can also list an available position. Call Joanne Jackson at (800) 955-3565 or write to her at this address: American Medical Association, 515 N. State Street, Chicago, IL 60610.

Appendix C:
State Medical Placement Offices

Alaska State Medical Association
1135 West 8th Avenue
Anchorage, AK 99501

Arizona Medical Association
810 West Bethany Home Road
Phoenix, AZ 85013

Arkansas Medical Society
#10 Corporate Hill Drive
P.O. Box 5776
Little Rock, AR 72215

California Medical Association
731 Market Street
San Francisco, CA 94103

Colorado Medical Society
P.O. Box 17550
Denver, CO 80217-0550

Connecticut State Medical Society
160 St. Ronan Street
New Haven, CT 06511

Florida Medical Association
760 Riverside Avenue
P.O. Box 2411
Jacksonville, FL 32203

Hawaii Medical Association
320 Ward Avenue, Suite 200
Honolulu, HI 96814

Idaho Medical Association
407 West Bannock Street
Boise, ID 83702

Illinois State Medical Society
Twenty North Michigan Ave., Suite 700
Chicago, IL 60602

Indiana State Medical Association
3935 North Meridian
Indianapolis, IN 46208

Iowa Medical Society
1001 Grand Avenue
West Des Moines, IA 50265

Kansas Medical Society
1300 Topeka Avenue
Topeka, KS 66612

Kentucky Medical Association
3532 Ephraim McDowell Drive
Louisville, KY 40205

Louisiana State Medical Society
1700 Josephine Street
New Orleans, LA 70113

Maine Medical Association
P.O. Box 190
Manchester, ME 04351

Massachusetts Medical Society
22 The Fenway
Boston, MA 02215

Medical Association of Georgia
983 Peachtree Street N.E.
Atlanta, GA 30309

Medical Association of the State of Alabama
19 South Jackson Street
Montgomery, AL 36197

Medical and Chirurgical Faculty of Maryland
1211 Cathedral Street
Baltimore, MD 21201

Medical Society of Delaware
1925 Lovering Avenue
Wilmington, DE 19806

Medical Society of the State of New York
420 Lakeville Road
Lake Success, NY 11042

Medical Society of Virginia
4205 Dover Road
Richmond, VA 23221

Michigan State Medical Society
120 West Saginaw Street
East Lansing, MI 48826-0950

Minnesota State Medical Association
2221 University Avenue
Suite 400
Minneapolis, MN 55414

Mississippi State Medical Association
735 Riverside Drive
Jackson, MS 39202

Missouri State Medical Association
113 Madison Street
Jefferson City, MO 65101

Montana Medical Association
2021 11th Avenue, Suite 12
Helena, MT 59601

Nebraska Medical Association
1512 Firstier Bank Building
Lincoln, NE 68508

Nevada State Medical Association
3660 Baker Lane, #101
Reno, NV 89509

New Hampshire Medical Society
4 Park Street
Concord, NH 03301

New Mexico Medical Society
2650 Yale Boulevard S.E.
Albuquerque, NM 87106

North Carolina Medical Society
P.O. Box 3910
Duke University Medical Center
Durham, NC 27710

North Dakota Medical Association
Box 1198
Bismarck, ND 58501

Ohio State Medical Association
4015 Executive Park Drive
Suite 304
Cincinnati, OH 45241

Oklahoma State Medical Association
601 N.W. Expressway
Oklahoma City, OK 73118

Oregon Medical Association
5210 West Corbett Street
Portland, OR 97201

Pennsylvania Medical Society
20 Erford Road
Lemoyne, PA 17043

Rhode Island Medical Society
106 Francis Street
Providence, RI 02903

South Carolina Medical Association
Box 11188
Columbia, SC 29211

South Dakota State Medical Association
608 West Avenue N
Sioux Falls, SD 57104

State Medical Society of Wisconsin
330 East Lakeside Street
Madison, WI 53701

Tennessee Medical Association
112 Louise Avenue
Nashville, TN 37203

Texas Medical Association
1801 North Lamar Boulevard
Austin, TX 78701

Utah State Medical Association
540 East 5th Street, S
Salt Lake City, UT 84102

Vermont State Medical Society
136 Main Street
Rutland, VT 05602

Washington State Medical Association
2033 Sixth Avenue
Seattle, WA 98121

West Virginia State Medical Association
4307 McCorkle Ave., S.E.
Charleston, WV 25304

Wyoming State Medical Society
1920 Evans Street
P.O. Drawer 4009
Cheyenne, WY 82001

To advertise in the following western states, contact:

Western Journal of Medicine
P.O. Box 7602
San Francisco, CA 94120-7602
(415) 882-5179

Representing:

Arizona Medical Association
California Medical Association
Idaho Medical Association
Nevada State Medical Association
New Mexico Medical Society
Utah Medical Association
Washington State Medical Association
Wyoming Medical Association

To advertise in the following states' journals*, contact:

The State Medical Journal Advertising Bureau, Inc.
711 South Boulevard
Oak Park, IL 60302
(708) 383-8800

Representing:

Alabama Medicine
Alaska Medicine
Arkansas Medical Society
Chicago Medicine
Connecticut Medicine
Delaware Medical Journal

---

*Display advertising only. No classified advertising. Classified advertising must be placed with the individual journal.

Florida Medical Association
Medical Association of Georgia
Hawaii Medical Journal
Indiana Medicine
Iowa Medicine
Kansas Medicine
Kentucky Medical Association
Louisiana State Medical Society
Maryland Medical Journal
Michigan Medicine
Minnesota Medicine
Mississippi State Medical Association
Missouri Medicine
Nebraska Medical Journal
North Carolina Medical Journal
Oklahoma State Medical Association
Rhode Island Medicine
South Carolina Medical Association
South Dakota Medicine
Tennessee Medical Association
Texas Medicine
Virginia Medical
West Virginia Medicine
Wisconsin Medicine

Appendix D:
Journals and Medical Publications

Internist
American Society of Internal Medicine
1101 Vermont Avenue N.W., Suite 500
Washington, DC 20005-3457

Journal of the American Medical Association
Classified Advertising
515 N. State Street
Chicago, IL 60610
(312) 464-5000

Military Medicine
Association of Military Surgeons of the U.S.
9320 Old Georgetown Road
Bethesda, MD 20814
(301) 897-8800

New England Journal of Medicine
Classified Advertising Sales
1440 Main Street
Waltham, MA 02154-1649
(617) 893-3800

Index